Finding Old Thatch

Victoria Connelly

Cover design by Celia Hart
Photos copyright © Roy Connelly and Victoria Connelly

Published by Suffolk Bunch
an imprint of Cuthland Press

ISBN: 978-1-910522-19-6

To Roy – thank you for finding Old Thatch!

Table of Contents

A New Arrival

I'm addicted to storytelling and, to me, the novel is the perfect form. But, a few years ago, when we were leaving the London suburbs to move to a cottage in rural Suffolk, I knew I had to write about the experience. After all, I grew up reading escape stories, lapping up the experiences of people who had given up their lives in the city to run a smallholding in the Welsh mountains or to live with an otter in the Scottish Highlands. It was a fun way to explore how I was feeling at the time and so, when we made the decision to sell Mulberry Cottage after nine happy years there, I thought it might be fun to write about it all.

Since the last Mulberry Cottage book was published, there have been a few new faces joining our little family and quite a few departures. In October 2014, we said a sad goodbye to our first dog, Molly. Molly was a Springer Spaniel/English Setter cross and we rescued her from a small animal shelter in Berkshire while we were living in London. She was around two or three years old and we were told that she had been kept on a farm in Ireland, chained to a gate and left outside in all weathers and, judging by her reaction to our first trip to the local park, she hadn't been socialised at all. She was terrified of almost every other dog that tried to approach her, barking her head off. But she adored people and gradually learned to make friends with her canine companions, and even had a few boyfriends whom she'd skip around in flirty fashion.

When we made the move from London to Suffolk, I couldn't wait to share the countryside footpaths with Molly because, apart from days out and holidays, she had known nothing but the suburban alleys and a litter-strewn park for her walks. Together we explored miles of footpaths, discovering local woods, valleys, riverside walks and sticky winter fields. She was our companion for ten years, and it broke our hearts to say goodbye to her.

It was on a sunny day in October when the vet visited our cottage. Molly had grown weaker and less able to take care of herself. Eating had become a huge issue and yet she still enjoyed her walks each day, her face lighting up as she rounded us up each morning and afternoon. We knew that she was physically deteriorating, but she adored nothing more than venturing out into our meadow, sniffing the scents of the wild animals and feeling the wind rippling through that long black and white fur of hers. But the day came when we knew it was time to say goodbye.

When we lost Molly, the pain was so intense that I vowed never to have an only dog again because the void she left behind was too awful. For a while, we didn't quite know what to do. We were heading towards winter and it didn't seem an ideal time to look for a puppy as toilet training in a muddy cold garden would not be easy or enjoyable for either the puppy or for us. But it wasn't long before I started researching local breeders of spaniels. It's funny when a certain breed of dog gets a hold of you, and we had truly fallen under the spell of spaniels and, although I've always loved to rescue animals, the pull of having a puppy was very strong.

We soon found a reputable breeder up near the Suffolk coast and went along to meet her and Izzie, the potential mother of some pups. We immediately fell in love with Izzie's gentle temperament, hoping that our future companion was safely growing in her womb. A few weeks later, we found out that Izzie was indeed having puppies and, in March, six were born: four dogs and two bitches.

That first visit to meet the puppies was so exciting. Our Hattie was just eight days old and was no bigger than a hamster. We visited every other week which seemed agonising to us and we wished we lived closer so that we could see her every day and watch her progress.

The second visit, when Hattie was just three weeks old, was a particularly memorable one for me. Her eyes had just opened, but she was still such a sleepy baby and happy to be held in my arms, docile and warm against my chin. It was a lovely moment. Then we visited her at five weeks' old. What a difference two weeks had made. She was a little live wire, running around the playroom, giving little barks and wriggling in our arms when we picked her up. And she hasn't stopped moving since that day.

Springer Spaniels are highly energetic dogs and Hattie has definitely kept us fit over the years. When we first brought her home, we didn't know what had hit us. We had never had a puppy before but how hard could it be? Well, we soon found out. It was absolutely exhausting. We'd decided to crate train her, creating a safe space she could call her own and, after a rather traumatic first night of her being away from her family where she whined for hours, she adapted and slept well.

We also erected a playpen in the living room so that we could leave her in safety while we cooked meals and went about our work. Alas, it only took Hattie about a day before she discovered that she could climb out of the playpen quite easily.

Like all puppies, Hattie explored the world with her mouth. She chewed everything and made a particular mess of one of our lovely old wooden chairs which still bears her teeth marks today. She pulled the braiding off another chair, ripped pieces of carpet up, and demolished many of her toys in record time.

And then there were the blissful moments when she would just collapse into sleep for around forty minutes. It was during these brief windows that Roy and I would race around and try and get some work done. But we both kind of knew this wasn't sustainable and so we decided it was best for all parties if we handed Hattie over to a local dog walker for three mornings a week. Although we felt slightly guilty about this, we just hadn't been getting enough work done and we were missing our old routine.

They say you should be careful what you wish for and we had chosen a pedigree Springer Spaniel who was full of energy and enthusiasm for life. Whenever we met somebody with a Springer, they would inevitably tell us that she would calm down in say three or four years' time. We would laugh – anxiously.

The first puppy training class we attended was in a nearby

village hall. Hattie was the only spaniel and we watched as the teacher instructed each owner to let go of their dog's lead. I think the idea was that your dog stayed by your side, and Roy and I felt pretty sure what would happen if we dropped Hattie's lead. When our turn came and we were asked to let Hattie's lead drop, we told the trainer what would happen, but she insisted. Sure enough, lead dropped, Hattie took off, racing around the room, sniffing all the new smells and revelling in the taste of freedom in this new space. There was also the added chaos of everyone calling Hattie's name and trying to catch her. The teacher wasn't happy and shouted at us and it was then that we knew we wouldn't be returning to that particular class again.

The next dog training class we found was held in a field which seemed like a much better option. It felt more real. After all, the really tricky stuff with Hattie took place outside. Once again, we had the only Springer Spaniel and, while we enjoyed meeting all the other dogs and getting Hattie socialised, the trainer didn't really know what to do with her and we never got her walking to heel there. We have since spoken to other spaniel owners who have attended similar classes and they said exactly the same thing.

When Hattie reached six months and was quite a handful, a friend recommended looking at gun dog trainers. Now, I'm the very last person on the planet who would want to use my dog for shooting, but the trainer we found knew the spaniel temperament and had her walking to heel within about ten minutes, although the shock he gave Hattie – which involved shouting, pulling on the lead and stomping all at once – still ricochets through us today, and was something we found impossible to do ourselves. Of course, this meant that she walked nicely to heel with the trainer, and watching her do so reminded us of a horse doing dressage but, as soon as she was handed to us, she pulled on the lead again.

Hattie still goes to training – this time with a class run by a man who knows his way around a gun dog and knows the sort of things they respond well to. At six years old, she is still a work in progress, but mainly because that's exactly what we are too.

There was one incident quite early on which we'll never forget. We had bought Hattie a long training lead and were walking along a footpath with fields either side when we noticed another dog coming towards us. Hattie, who loves greeting all other people and most other dogs, got incredibly excited and started running towards the other dog. I panicked and grabbed hold of the long training lead which whipped through my fingers causing immense pain. Within ten minutes, my fingers had begun to swell up alarmingly and what was most worrying was that it was my left hand and I was wearing both my wedding ring and engagement ring. It soon became impossible to take my rings off and we began to wonder if we should have the rings cut off, but I really didn't want this to happen because I had always worn my wedding ring, never taking it off since the moment Roy had placed it on my finger on our wedding day. So I applied ice, kept my hand raised and hoped for the best.

This was on the twenty-third of December and I remember it well because I had a dental appointment for root canal on Christmas Eve at nine in the morning. It was the only appointment they had and I had grabbed it because I was so terrified that things would flare up over Christmas and I wouldn't be able to be seen then. So I sat down in the dentist's chair, my fingers still horribly swollen and a rather startling shade of blue now, and the dentist clapped his eyes on my hand and shrieked in horror.

'You've *got* to have those rings cut off right away! Promise me!' he said and I nodded helplessly. So, on Christmas Eve, having just had root canal surgery, I stumbled into town to find the nearest jeweller and watched as my beloved rings were cut free from my swollen finger. I felt extremely sorry for myself that day and it would be more than a year before my finger recovered fully and I was able to have my rings mended so that I could wear them again.

Another moment in Hattie's puppyhood that we'll never forget was her first public engagement after she'd had all her jabs. It was to visit an artist's garden and open studio. It belonged to a sculptor and the garden was full of enormous bronzes, including one of a wolf that terrified Hattie. We walked around the garden and then headed into the studio to meet the sculptor, asking if it was okay if Hattie came in with us. The artist had two large dogs of her own and Hattie was made a great fuss of. Unfortunately, all the excitement got a bit too much and Hattie decided that she had to go to the toilet right there and then in the middle of the studio floor. Luckily, we had a dog poop bag and were able to clean it up swiftly and the artist thought it was incredibly funny. We thanked our lucky stars that the floor was a concrete one and that Hattie's little accident helped remember us to the artist who has her own gallery and who promptly invited Roy to exhibit his paintings there in a show.

But we didn't take Hattie to any more artists' studios for a while.

The Hens of Mulberry Cottage

We have been so lucky with the garden here at Mulberry Cottage. It's formed in sections and the first part of the back garden is naturally enclosed by what we call the 'spooky shed' – a long wooden shed which is rather dilapidated, but has plenty of character as well as cobwebs, and looks like something out of a Beatrix Potter story. Along with the back of the house and two large hedges, this has made the perfect garden for hens and means that we can watch them from the kitchen and landing windows.

The last flock of ex-battery hens to arrive at Mulberry Cottage were all named after Shakespearean heroines: Beatrice, Rosalind, Viola and Hermia. They arrived pretty much as all the ex-bats do with most of their feathers missing. Viola and Hermia were particularly bald and the dear things loved nothing more than to sunbathe. This worried me greatly and I spent a good deal of that summer chasing them around the garden and applying sunscreen to their bald spots.

I have to say that this little flock was a rather troublesome one in terms of health. We had so many trips to the vets, which is always traumatic not only for the hen but for us too. And we came to the painful decision, after the last of this flock died, to have a rest from ex-bats for a while. We had been keeping them for eight years and they'd been such a delight and we would definitely rescue more in the future because I couldn't imagine my life without rescuing things. But we'd have a little break first.

Of course, deciding not to have hens for a while is one thing, but it's quite another to look out into the garden and not see a hen preening on a low wall or one dust bathing under a rose bush. The garden seemed so bleak and empty without them and so we decided to treat ourselves and look into getting some really posh hens. I'd been a bit obsessed with Buff Orpingtons since seeing them photographed so beautifully by the writer, Francine Raymond. She had a flock in her Suffolk garden for years and they were absolutely gorgeous – great golden girls, almost round like feathery footballs, strutting around her garden with voluptuous grace. I knew I wanted at least one of these in our new flock and so we found a breeder – the same breeder, it turned out, who Francine had got her hens from.

It was so exciting to visit and see the hens he had and, after much deliberation because they really were all so beautiful, we settled on a Buff Orpington, a Black Orpington and a Blue Partridge Brahma. I'll never forget the moment when the breeder grabbed hold of the Brahma and placed her in my arms. Even though she was a point of lay hen, so just about to start laying eggs and still quite young, she was huge and heavy and very docile. I couldn't quite believe that I was going to be the caretaker of this wonderful creature, and I couldn't wait to get the pretty trio home.

Sticking with Shakespearean names, I called the Buff Orpington Portia from *The Merchant of Venice*, the Black Orpington was Phoebe, named after a character in *As You Like It*, and the Brahma was named Perdita from *The Winter's Tale*.

I'd been discovering a lot about Buff Orpingtons. They were a favourite breed of the late Queen Mother and, reading one of Francine Raymond's books, I laughed out loud when she wrote that Buff Orpingtons were most definitely pets and not to be kept for meat because it would be like eating the pet Labrador. How right she was. They are definitely one of the most beautiful hens I have ever seen.

Another well-known fact about Buff Orpingtons is that they can get broody, and it was the following spring when we witnessed this first-hand with Portia. One day, we discovered that she was sitting in the nest box for an incredibly long time, longer than it would take to lay an egg. Was this it, we wondered? Was this a broody hen?

We observed her for a few days and, by this time, she had amassed half a dozen eggs underneath her, and was only coming out once a day to drink and feed. She had also been plucking the feathers on her breast, making a neat nest around her.

We talked it over with a farmer friend. Yes, we definitely had a broody hen on our hands, she told us, lamenting because her own hens weren't broody and they were in need of some new stock.

We didn't link the two things together at once. It was only later when our friend suggested that we take some of her eggs, which would probably be fertile thanks to her cockerel, and place them under Portia, replacing the ones she was currently sitting on which would never hatch as we didn't have a cockerel. But we didn't have a place for Portia to hatch her eggs and raise chicks away from the other hens. No problem, our friend said, telling us they had a broody coop we could borrow. Roy and I looked at each other. Should we? *Could* we? The thought of having chicks in the spring at Mulberry Cottage was just too tempting. I tried to imagine our beautiful Portia becoming a mother hen and my heart just melted.

'Yes, please,' we told our friend.

The broody coop was soon delivered and installed in the hen garden and, after making a few repairs to the holes in the roof, we waited for dark, when chickens are sleepy and easy to handle. Not that our Portia was difficult; she was one of the most docile hens I've ever encountered. But, broody hens can be quite defensive of their precious eggs, so it was as well to play things safe. We'd put bedding into the broody coop and had gently placed the nine eggs from the farm in the nest. And then we went to get Portia, scooping her up from the eggs she had gathered and placing her gently onto the farm eggs in the broody coop.

We were like a couple of mother hens ourselves after that, watching Portia constantly and making sure she was feeding and drinking. We even panicked about the eggs when she left them oh-so-briefly, placing a woolly hat over them while she fed and drank. We also made sure that the eggs were regularly turned, although we could see Portia was doing this herself. But it's an important job – otherwise the developing embryo can stick to the membrane and the chick could hatch malformed.

We knew we had to wait a whole twenty-one days before the

eggs would hatch and the waiting was agony. Would they all hatch? Were the eggs even fertilised? Would they all be cockerels? And would Portia know what to do?

Before twenty-one days had elapsed, we noticed that one of the eggs wasn't looking healthy. It was darker than the others and looked as though it might be rotting inside and so we took it away. Eight eggs remained. Eight potential new lives. It was so exciting.

We'll never forget hearing those first tiny cheeps as the eggs began to hatch. For a little while, Portia's chicks hid under her and so it was hard to tell just how many chicks there were as we didn't want to disturb them. But we soon discovered that all eight eggs had hatched and Portia was so gentle, not only with her chicks, but with us too. We had read that mother hens can be incredibly defensive and might attack anyone who approaches their chicks. Not so with Portia. She didn't mind us saying hello although we were careful not to disturb her too often. But this was our first flock of chicks and we couldn't resist cupping them in our hands, their little fluffy bodies as light as air. Eight little beauties. At this stage, we didn't know how many were hens and how many cockerels. The ratio can be as high as half and half, but we had made sure that we had an understanding with our farmer friend, and she was to take all the cockerels back as well as half of the hens, for we couldn't resist keeping some ourselves.

For a few weeks, the chicks all looked alike bar two. Six of them were that wonderful yolky-yellow that you see depicted on everything from chocolate eggs to fine china around Easter time. But there was one that was a shade darker. In fact, she was the exact same colour as our Portia. Another had glorious black and white colouring and we quickly named it Marble.

Portia was the perfect mother, gathering her chicks around her and showing them how to feed, and calling to them if a predator flew over the garden. We saw this in action one day. They were all in the run together, pecking around and playing when Portia suddenly let out a cry as a bird flew overhead. It was probably nothing more than a pigeon, but the chicks instantly ran for cover.

But then tragedy struck. Chicks are so tiny and vulnerable and they move around at incredible speed, but not always with a sense of direction and purpose, and it was as we were opening the pop hole one morning to the now familiar explosion of chicks that dear Portia accidentally stepped on one as it ran in front of her. We didn't think much of it at first until we noticed one chick looking quite sorry for itself. We kept an eye on it before bringing it inside, where we made sure it was warm and had access to food and water, but it faded fast and we lost it. It was heartbreaking. We felt so helpless. This dear little life that had had so much potential.

As they got bigger and bolder, the seven remaining chicks discovered jumping and something they particularly liked to jump on top of was Portia. They loved riding on her and we delighted in watching them jump up onto her back. This was fine when they were little, but Portia tired of it when they got bigger and would make sure they dropped off her quickly.

It soon became obvious that three of the chicks were cockerels. We were able to tell because their combs grew so much bigger than those of the hens. They also seemed to make slightly more noise than the hens and we realised that we would have to take them to the farm in the near future. Because there were four hens, we were going to keep two of them and send two back to the farm with the three cockerels, but it was a wrench to see them go and, yes, we had named them all! Portia was much better at parting with them than we were. One day, we saw her clucking and pacing in the run, intent on getting back out into the garden with her grown-up friends. She had raised her brood and now wanted her old life back.

So, one day, we packed the two young hens and three young cockerels into two boxes, popped them in the back of the car and drove to the farm. Our friend was delighted with them and we were thrilled to keep two hens ourselves to merge with our current flock.

Keeping up with the Shakespearean names, we called the white hen Audrey after the shepherdess in *As You Like It*, and the little golden hen was going to be called Olivia from *Twelfth Night*, but we'd already started calling her Mini P as she looked so like Portia, who could easily be her birth mother instead of her surrogate one.

Audrey and Mini P became a natural pair, slowly merging into the flock and learning to enjoy all that their new home had to offer. Audrey, in particular, loved to jump onto a bench we had outside our back door. From there, she could peep into the conservatory where she knew the corn was kept. And Mini P became a star layer, giving us the biggest, roundest eggs I have ever seen. It was a joy to have them as part of the family and we were so pleased to have experienced hatching and raising our own chicks.

Apple Orchards

We've been very lucky in the time we've lived at Mulberry Cottage to have had access onto land beyond the end of our meadow. It's privately owned and includes a small lake and a very large apple orchard. Walking here means we don't have to cross any roads. It's safe and secure and both Molly and Hattie have been able to run free off lead.

At its height, this special place was a paradise especially in late spring when the blossom would bloom palest pink and white against clear blue skies, and the deeper pinks of special pollinator trees looked particularly lovely. I loved watching the bees dancing among it all and the confetti showers of petals when the wind blew.

But the passing years changed this little Eden and we were saddened to hear the news that the owner had died. Not long beforehand, he had sold a portion of the land to a local developer who immediately fenced off a great section so we weren't able to walk across it anymore. He then opened it up as a caravan park and it wasn't long before he applied for planning permission to build houses on the land.

Still, we had the lake and much of the orchard left to walk through although, since the owner had died, it hadn't been maintained. Slowly, nature took over, swallowing up the path with nettles and thistles. The trees gradually died, woefully nibbled by deer and rabbits. It was sad to watch the decline but, as I walked around with Hattie during our final year, I noticed how very few of the trees blossomed in the spring and gave fruit in the autumn. I couldn't help wondering what would happen to this place, but I feared that it would all be bought by the developer sooner rather than later and that it wouldn't be long before houses were built here with new cul-de-sacs leading to them with names like Orchard Way and Apple Tree View, only the trees will be long gone.

Nothing stays the same for long, not even in the country, and it isn't just cities and towns that are developed. So much of our countryside is being swallowed up and, once it's gone, it's very hard to get it back.

A New Life Beckons

Change is never easy, but we knew it was coming. After nine years at Mulberry Cottage, we felt it was time to move on. Moving here after eleven years in the noisy London suburbs was the best thing we'd ever done, but life in our little village was rapidly changing. Pockets of land had been sold for development and we were slowly becoming enclosed just as we had been in the London suburbs, with views being lost and noise levels rising. In short, it was no longer the village that we had chosen to move to. Things had changed and it was time for us to have a change too.

Of course, trying to move house in the middle of a global pandemic and a national recession wasn't perhaps the best idea we'd ever had. But, when you make your mind up to do something, it's hard not to follow through and so we put our house on the market and started looking for a new home.

It was going to be hard saying goodbye. We had written so many books here, painted so many paintings, rescued an awful lot of hens, said goodbye to our dear Molly and welcomed our first puppy, Hattie. We had made a beautiful home that suited us too: ripping out the rather nasty 1970s fireplace to reveal the two-hundred-year-old one and installing a wood burner. This really had become the heart of our home for gatherings with friends and lazy evenings watching films or reading books. So much life had been lived here. Could we really leave it now?

Of course, no place is perfect and, although Mulberry Cottage had a wonderful garden, it was very much overlooked and, as much as we loved our two sets of neighbours, they would sometimes hold conversations with each other right across our garden. This lack of privacy is quite hard when you're an introvert as I am, and then there were the practical issues like not being able to sneak into the garden in your nightie to let the hens out in the morning or to check on the greenhouse. When I'm in my garden, I like to think and dream and I don't necessarily want to have a conversation with somebody else. So our hope was to find a house with a bit more privacy and a wraparound garden with lots of little areas where you could sit in peace and quiet without being overlooked and where I could, at last, sneak out into the garden in my nightie to let the hens out.

House Viewings

We had actually started viewing properties in earnest a year before we put our house on the market. There really was very little around, but each one that we saw had something special about it and none more so than the house with the walled garden. Readers of my novels will know that I am a little bit obsessed with walled gardens. I have written a trilogy which features walled gardens and they also appear in a few of my other books too. They are such special places and it would be a dream come true for us to own one, but they usually come attached to very large manor houses with very big price tags. However, when a modest-sized property came onto the market with its very own walled garden, I knew we had to take a look at it.

The property was the coach house on the estate of a manor house, and other buildings like the old stables had been converted into homes as well. The property we were going to look at came with the walled garden. Could this be the place for us? The house itself looked a little small and the garden was completely overlooked by the big manor house, but could we compromise on privacy for the sake of owning a walled garden?

There was something else that was a bit special about this particular wall. It was what's known as a crinkle crankle wall – that is a wavy or serpentine shape. They are peculiar to East Anglia and are very rare so it would be an extraordinary thing to own. And it was lovely. I would have been very happy growing my flowers and vegetables in such a beautiful place, but not only was the house small and overlooked, but it was awfully close to a main road which was very noisy. As soon as you opened the door to exit the property, you were enveloped in traffic noise. It was too high a price to pay and it would have detracted from the peace you should enjoy in a garden.

Another property that looked great on paper was one up near the Suffolk and Norfolk border, just down the lane from where composer Benjamin Britten had his country bolthole. Having been brought up in Norfolk, I do have a special love of this county and knew you could get a bargain in certain parts of it. But the property we viewed really was in the middle of nowhere and despite having a marvellous vinery boasting juicy grapes and an outdoor swimming pool, we realised that we'd be cutting ourselves off from a lot of life if we moved there.

Then there was a sweet little place which looked very much like a larger version of Mulberry Cottage. A pretty front garden greeted us and a tiled porch and hallway made us smile, knowing how wonderfully practical this would be for us Springer Spaniel owners, but the back garden was woefully small. In fact, half of it had been sold by the current owners and a new house built upon it.

After viewing this cottage, we drove to the nearest church, which I had long wanted to see, and we sat in the car as it began to rain. It was a shame that this cottage and its garden wasn't right for us as the village was lovely and it was surrounded by very pretty countryside, but there was no way we could squash ourselves, our spaniel, the hens and all the raised beds, greenhouses and polytunnels that we wanted into it.

And that seemed to be the main issue we had with the properties which were coming onto the market. There were some real beauties, but they all lacked a good-sized garden. We had been thoroughly spoilt at Mulberry Cottage and we really didn't want to give up having all that space. Another house we visited, had a beautiful garden full of fruit trees, raised beds and rambling roses but, unfortunately, it was overlooked by a footpath that ran down one side of it. I wouldn't have been able to dig up my veggies in my nightie there.

And then there was Church House – a fifteenth-century building in a tiny village south of Bury St Edmunds, overlooking one of Suffolk's most glorious brick and flint churches. Painted pink, with white-framed casement windows and an enormous wooden front door, it took our breath away on a sultry day in August after a week-long heatwave. The sky was achingly blue, and house martins chatted happily as they flew in and out of the nests under the eaves. The rooms were large and characterful with enormous inglenook fireplaces and two very impressive wooden staircases. The main room at the top of house was like a cathedral with its soaring beams. There were plenty of outbuildings too. But the garden! Could we really squash ourselves into it? Could I kiss goodbye to my polytunnel dreams? Could I be just as happy with slightly fewer flowers?

The clincher came as we were standing outside in the sunshine, looking up at the glorious façade of the Grade 2 listed house. 'Full disclosure,' the estate agent said. 'There's no central heating.' He mentioned it so casually as if it was no big deal. Roy and I stared at each other. How had we missed that? It is truly remarkable what you *don't* see when viewing a property for the first time. We had been so carried away by the romance of it all, by the mere thought of being custodians of such a special place, of giving it our gentle love, and of restoring the overgrown garden, that we had completely overlooked the fact that there were no radiators. We were so torn and told the estate agent that we would think about it.

We left the garden, crossing the track into the churchyard and gazing back at the house, framed now by Victorian gravestones and the long bleached grasses of summer. It looked like something out of a Merchant Ivory film – the kind the heroine would waft around in a beautiful dress that would rustle when the hero embraced her. We really couldn't make this one work, could we? *Could* we? As we walked around the church, marvelling at the flint flushwork, we listed the pros and cons, and the cons far outweighed the pros.

It truly hurt to leave that one and I do believe it stole a little piece of my heart, but perhaps I'll write about it one day. Perhaps one of my brave characters will live there and I can visit them in my mind whenever I want to. But I'll make sure I install central heating for them first.

Selling Mulberry Cottage

We handed in the paperwork at the estate agents on a Thursday afternoon at the end of July and the property appeared online on Friday. Seeing that 'for sale' board go up gave us mixed emotions. Very quickly, appointments were made to see the property and, rather surprisingly, somebody made an offer for the full asking price before even seeing it. Of course, I couldn't blame them because it is the kind of property that's easy to fall in love with at first sight, but it did feel a bit of a strange way to do business.

We had decided not to do first viewings ourselves. It was much easier if we scooted out with our Hattie and left the estate agent to it. Hattie is a very loving and enthusiastic dog and she adores nothing more than visitors, which can be a little overwhelming if you are not a dog fan. So we decided to make sure we didn't scare anybody off with our spaniel. We also closed the hens up in their covered run. Normally, they have full free-range of their garden, but not everybody would appreciate entering a garden full of hens running full pelt towards them. So we popped them away on the first morning of the viewings. They were not happy about this. Perdita took it particularly badly, pacing up and down, wanting to be let out, but at least it gave me a chance to do a quick tidy up of the lawn.

There were five viewings on that first day and three more appointments were made for the week after. On the Monday, we had a call from the estate agent to say that the couple who had originally offered the full asking price before even seeing the property had now seen it and wanted to go ahead. We were delighted and we soon got to meet them on their second viewing, taking our property off the market and cancelling the other appointments that had been made to view it now that we had a buyer.

It's an odd thing showing strangers around your home, knowing that they are going to live in it one day. But it was lovely to hear their comments. They were just as in love with it as we had been when we had viewed it all those years ago, and they marvelled at the garden, telling us their plans to keep their own hens and their ambition to have goats too.

We really hadn't expected to sell Mulberry Cottage so quickly and we became a little anxious because we still haven't found anywhere that suited us. Luckily, our buyers assured us that there was no rush. This was such a comfort to hear. Of course, I think it was everyone's unspoken aim to be in well before Christmas and to start the New Year in our respective new homes.

Three weeks went by in which Roy and I saw several properties, but it was the usual story of them not having gardens that suited us. And then we were told about a property by a friend of ours that might just be what we were looking for. And, indeed, it was.

It was Old Thatch.

With joy in our hearts, we rang our estate agent to tell him the good news. Unfortunately, he had some bad news for us. We had lost our buyers. From assuring us that they weren't in any rush, our buyers were suddenly now in the most awful rush and wanted to exchange by October which wasn't possible as we'd only just found Old Thatch. What was baffling to us was that they'd just booked their mortgage surveyor to come round later that week.

Obviously, that was now cancelled. It was all so frustrating as we'd just found our future home and were ready to make good progress now.

We had lost the whole of August to these buyers. The garden had looked wonderful and now it had that end of summer look – droopy and despondent – with the roses between flushes and the sunflowers past their best, and we were going back onto the market.

They say that moving house is one of the most stressful things you can go through and I never believe it until I'm in the midst of it. I always think it's going to be exciting and a total joy and then I remember that you have to deal with so many other people and that absolutely nothing is in your control.

Newbuild vs Oldbuild

One of the problems with old buildings is that they don't score too highly when it comes to being energy efficient. When it came to Mulberry Cottage being surveyed for its energy performance certificate, I could have saved the man a job. We knew that we would be classed as 'E'. Virtually every property we took a liking to was classed as being 'E' or, in the case of Church House, it was exempt from being tested because it was so ancient and draughty or, in other words, historically important.

When we first came to Mulberry Cottage, it was very cold. We had moved in at the end of November when it was dark by four o'clock. There was a small fireplace in the sitting room, but you had to be sitting almost on top of it to feel any heat. They say that up to ninety percent of an open fire's heat goes up the chimney rather than out into the room and we could easily believe that. So we decided to do something about it, knocking the 1970s fireplace out to reveal the two hundred-year-old one behind it and installing an efficient wood burning stove. We also insulated the attic. It all made a huge difference and we were soon cosy in our cottage.

When we were looking at properties, we were always drawn to older ones and, very often, the older the better because they were so full of character. I suppose, if we had really wanted something that came with mod cons, we'd have bought a newbuild, but we really didn't want box rooms that all looked identical. We actually rather like the odd bulging wall or sloping floor boards. The fact is, we love historic buildings.

Another thing about modern homes is that they often come with tiny gardens. That wouldn't have suited us at all. We need space around us for our free-ranging hens, our energetic spaniel, our fruit trees, our flower beds, greenhouses and polytunnels. We were open to a characterful eco-house that had a good plot of land, but we just never found one and so resigned ourselves to wearing thick woollies and thermals to see us through the winters.

Older buildings can be tricky to live in. We were so used to double-glazed windows and, although Mulberry Cottage wasn't the most energy efficient property ever, we hadn't been cold in it since making our improvements and we knew we were going to miss the woodburner. Old Thatch has two enormous fireplaces, but only one was working and, when we moved in, we knew it would need inspecting before we'd feel safe using it.

Another thing about older properties is that they are often listed, and Old Thatch is a Grade II. This is something I feel very proud of, but I realised that it could hamper any improvements we wanted to make, as any work you want to do on a listed property needs listed building consent and planning permission which takes time and patience. This was new territory for us. Life had been easy at Mulberry Cottage. If we wanted to repaint or rip a fireplace out, we could just go right ahead. But the rules for listed properties are vital because these wonderful old buildings should be protected.

Old Thatch

We had never set out to buy a timber-framed thatched cottage. Although I'd fallen in love with a pink thatched cottage where I had house-sat for an artist friend one summer, we had never gone in search of one ourselves. But it's funny how life works out and you may have the most comprehensive shopping list in the world, but then something unexpected happens and your heart is stolen.

It came about in an unusual way. I had been looking for properties on Rightmove for the last two or three years, and we'd viewed a fair few. Roy had left the job of making shortlists to me and I was happy to take that on. After all, I am a writer and one of the necessary traits of a writer is nosiness and it was so much fun looking for properties online.

Then, one day, after coming home from painting a harvest scene in the local fields, Roy said that he'd spoken to a friend in the village, mentioning that we were looking for a new home and she'd casually said that her daughter was thinking of putting her house on the market. It was in a nearby village. In fact, it was only about a mile away from one of our favourite villages in Suffolk where we'd already viewed one property before. I began to get excited. Our friend told us that her daughter and her family were away that weekend and that we were welcome to go and look around the garden to get a feel for the place and see if it was right for us.

The next day, we drove out there, excitement bubbling inside as we parked beside a low brick and flint wall and gasped at the thatched cottage. We got out of the car and made our way around the garden, noting the wisteria which was in flower, smiling at the friendly dormer windows set under the thatch. It was having its ridge rethatched and there were blond reeds cascading down the chocolate-coloured roof and onto the garden below. It was well-detached with the wraparound garden we had been looking for and there were fruit trees, a greenhouse, a herb garden and views across fields at the back.

By the time we got back to the car, Hattie, who had come with us, was more than ready for a walk and we took off through the village, heading down a lane into the valley, passing a couple of people out with their own dogs. Could these be future neighbours and future friends, we wondered?

The landscape was lush, full of trees in their summer finery and cows grazing happily. We skirted a field which opened out onto a recently harvested corn field with views back towards the village. There was a feeling of openness there and it was so very peaceful. We liked this place. This could be home.

The next week, we made an appointment with the owner to view the cottage properly and there it was again: that bubble of excitement when something just feels right. It began in the kitchen which was exactly what I'd been looking for. It was large and square with plenty of room for a breakfast table. There were three windows – one looking out over the back garden and two across the front garden. There was also a shiny royal blue Aga, just the kind that I gave to my beloved characters Robyn and Dan at Horseshoe Cottage in the Austen Addicts books. It was quite heady to think that I might be cooking on it in just a few short months.

The kitchen led on to a dining room with impressive stud walls and an enormous inglenook fireplace. The living room was similarly wonderful with beams, stud walls and another large fireplace and lots of little windows looking out onto the garden. It was very easy to imagine sitting in this room by the fire, a book in my hands and our dog by my feet.

I have always found it hard to hide my emotions when viewing a property. If I genuinely love something, I tend to gush about it and this was the first house we'd viewed that we could really imagine living in. I'd already planted half the garden and installed the chickens, and we were trying to work out where we would put our larger pieces of furniture and which rooms would be used for which purpose.

I had always joked about Mulberry Cottage being modern by Suffolk standards in that it was only two hundred years old. Well, Old Thatch was more than twice as old as Mulberry Cottage. I also regularly suffered from a disposition I refer to as "beam envy" when visiting older properties. Now, I would have more beams and stud walls than any person has a right to.

If we could afford it.

Old Thatch wasn't on the market with an estate agent, but the owners had an idea of its value. Of course, we did too and ours was lower than theirs so we decided to get it valued by a well-respected independent surveyor. Once we received his valuation, we put in an offer. There was a little back and forth negotiating, but we very quickly agreed on a price. We were going to buy a thatched cottage!

It was on a warm sunny day in September when we viewed Old Thatch for the second time and both of the owners were there to greet us. We spent over two hours with them, asking questions and being shown every beautiful, characterful inch of the property. They pointed out each of the fruit trees and we were delighted to discover that not only were there varieties of apple, but also a number of cherry trees, plums and a walnut. And we watched in awe as the thatcher worked up on the ridge. The pattern he was creating was evident this time and it looked so very neat and precise. Every so often, he'd climb down from the roof and walk across the garden to make sure that he had everything just as he wanted it.

It's quite incredible what you miss on the first viewing and then spot on the second and we realised just how very low the ceilings were at Old Thatch and there were beams to consider as well. When going through two of the doors, you had to duck to avoid banging your head. So where was our longcase clock going to go? Would my bookcases fit in the room I'd earmarked for my study up in the eaves? Although we'd lived in an old cottage for the last nine years, we'd been incredibly lucky that the taller ceilings were high enough for us, if not for some of our friends. It reminded me of a friend of ours who once moved into a cottage with low ceilings and had to saw off the bottom of her longcase clock so it would fit. I have to say that idea didn't appeal to me. Perhaps we'd have to cut a hole in the floor instead as we'd heard other people had done. Or perhaps we'd get lucky and it would fit snugly just where we wanted it to.

We continued our viewing, spending some time in the kitchen which I couldn't wait to cook in, and I watched as the owner leaned up against the Aga. When he saw me looking at him, he moved away to let me have a turn. Apparently, this was one of the great joys of owning an Aga – it was a great bottom warmer.

We left that day feeling happy and excited and counting down the days until we could call Old Thatch home. But we had our reservations too because we had never owned a listed property before nor one as old as this.

I have written a lot about old buildings in my novels from ancient priories to medieval manor houses and moated granges. I've always been fascinated by them. After graduating, I spent the summer working for the National Trust at Blickling Hall in Norfolk – a fine Tudor house which stands on the site of an earlier home which belonged to Anne Boleyn's family. I worked in the offices and as a room steward, soaking up the atmosphere of the beautiful rooms. But was I ready to actually own a little piece of England's history – even if it was on a much smaller scale?

I won't even tell you how many times we drove past Old Thatch over the next few weeks, keeping an eye on how the ridge was progressing. Every time I thought about it, I found that I was smiling – a big silly smile that filled my face and my heart. I had many concerns like would we be able to afford to heat it? Would there be repairs that we couldn't yet see? What would the full structural survey reveal? But I felt so perfectly content about it all too. This felt like the right thing to do – like an adventure we just had to go on.

Mulberry Cottage Takes a Stand

It was shortly after our buyers pulled out and Mulberry Cottage was back on the market, that strange things started happening. The boiler was the first to go. It was a pretty old model, probably the best part of thirty years old. It'd been in the back of our minds for years to replace it with something more energy efficient, but we had done that back in the London suburbs. There, we had been advised to take out a boiler that was a little old but which was running perfectly well, and replace it with a new condensing boiler. Well, I won't go into all the issues we had with that new one but, suffice to say, it was a nightmare and we wished we'd never pulled the old one out.

So, here we were, with our current boiler on the blink and hoping that a small part just needed replacing and that it hadn't died completely. Luckily, it was fixable, but a new pump was needed which had to be ordered from another part of the country.

In the meantime, our shower broke. So we had no hot water unless we boiled a kettle and couldn't use either the bath or the shower. Then, to compound things further, the kitchen tap went. It had been on the blink for a while and Roy did his best to fix it, but it really needed replacing so we made an appointment with a plumber. As the rest of Mulberry Cottage is on a water softener, this meant that we were now down to only one tap with drinkable water, and that was the garden tap.

It was a very interesting couple of days with the plumber visiting between house viewings and bills for nearly six hundred pounds at the end of it. It was almost as if our dear home was protesting, telling us not to leave and that it wasn't happy that we were trying to sell it to somebody else. A fanciful thought, perhaps, but that's what it felt like in the midst of all the problems we were having.

Everything for the Last Time

It's funny that, once you know you're going, there's this feeling of doing everything for the last time. There's the last time you'll celebrate Christmas in your home, the last time you'll see the spring garden rushing into bloom, the last time you'll walk in your neighbours' cherry orchard.

One of the most poignant moments was knowing that we were entering our last village show. It had been such a feature in our annual calendar and, at one stage, we thought it would be cancelled completely due to the Covid-19 pandemic. But the village rallied round and hired a marquee because the village hall was out of bounds, and a one-way system was set up for entries to be delivered. Everybody had done a marvellous job and there were some fabulous entries – from eye-wateringly large marrows to delicious cakes and jams, and beautiful floral displays.

We have felt so lucky to have a local village show. It was one of the surprise bonuses when we moved to Suffolk. I'd been watching every single episode of the River Cottage programmes and had dreamed of having a show like the ones Hugh Fearnley-Whittingstall entered in his Dorset village where you could win the much coveted 'vegetable cup'. And we haven't done too badly in the nine years we've been here. Both Roy and I have won the WI Shield for best exhibit in baking. I've won the art prize a couple of times for my photographs and, one year, I even won the best in show prize for my dahlias.

Will there be a village show where we are moving to? I will miss the friendly rivalry and excitement of when the doors open after judging and you get to see if your entries have been placed. I'll miss seeing the very best produce grown in the village, cleaned, primped and presented so proudly.

We were also going to miss our little allotment down at the nearby watermill. We had taken a couple of beds there after being persuaded by a friend. We really didn't need the extra room as we had quite enough to look after in our own garden, but it was such a special place in the heart of a secret valley alongside the village brook, that we couldn't say no. We also rather liked the idea of being a part of something like an allotment scheme. As it was privately owned, there was no rent to pay as such. Payment was roughly ten percent of the produce you grew so, over the few years we had it, we made payment in squashes, chard, tomatoes

and flowers, leaving them by the door of the mill house for the owner.

Another advantage of having an allotment is that you can see what others are growing and, with any luck, get lots of tips. We had the very good fortune of our little plot being alongside one of our village's best gardeners. He'd won many coveted prizes at our village show and we could now see why. His plot was immaculate and his produce had me gasping in wonder. I have never seen such neat rows of vegetables and his sunflowers towered over us, their stems as thick as our wrists. It was so inspiring and made you believe that the sky really was the limit, especially when it came to growing sunflowers.

The Ones We Leave Behind

I love the challenge of a new garden, planning how you will use the space, seeing all the possibilities, meeting and getting to know the resident plants, and looking forward to planting all your old favourites and introducing new varieties as well.

The autumn before we put our house on the market, I made sure I potted up most of my dahlias, not only because I wanted to protect them from the winter weather and any invading rabbits, but because there was no way I was going to leave these colourful friends behind after I'd spent hours carefully choosing them from gardening catalogues. I also took cuttings of rosemary and marjoram and dug up a wonderfully healthy clump of Welsh onion whose flowers are so beloved by the bees.

For a while, I wondered whether I should try and propagate the globe thistles which grow in profusion in the south-facing garden at Mulberry Cottage. I love their jolly round heads in that steely-blue shade, and they are another favourite of the bees, but I'm not so keen on their prickly leaves and the thought of getting in among them to secure a few plants for the new garden had me rapidly deciding that perhaps I could do without them. After all, I'd had nine years of joy looking at them and maybe I could grow some in the future from a nice safe packet of seeds.

But, oh, my roses! How was I going to leave all those behind?

Those of you who've read the Mulberry Cottage trilogy and my novel *The Rose Girls* will realise just how much I love my roses.

There were only a few rose bushes in the garden when we moved in, but I soon fixed that. Now, when I say *I* fixed that, I do of course mean Roy did, because he's the one who did the hard graft of digging over fifty holes in which to plant my beloved roses. But what fun it was choosing the varieties. I had so much fun creating our rose borders and, knowing that we were going, I attempted my first ever rose cuttings during the autumn and winter before we were planning to move, filling the conservatory windowsills with their funny, thorny stems. I'd heard that fifty percent of roses make it from cuttings and I was optimistic.

Cut to the following spring and I realised that there had been quite a few casualties. I was left with just four different varieties. A few weeks later, after gauging their progress, I deemed them strong and independent enough to pot up and was thrilled to discover we had ten new plants and, over the next few weeks, I watched as they grew and bloomed. What a joy it was to have created even more roses for the garden. I couldn't think why I hadn't made cuttings before. And at least I could take a few of my beauties with me now.

Come the following autumn, I decided that I really couldn't leave my beloved *Rosa Mundi* behind and, together with Roy, dug it up. It had been in the ground for nine years and really didn't want to budge, its spindly stems hiding its incredibly chunky main root. This old beauty had been with us a long time. I bought it for our home in London and refused to leave it behind there, so this would be its second move with us. But I was determined it was coming and watched in awe as Roy pulled it out of the ground. I quickly potted it up, not forgetting to label it, and delighted in the knowledge that we would be taking this stripy pink and white beauty with us.

For our first few years at Mulberry Cottage, the front garden path was a worn away concrete affair which wasn't attractive and definitely not what we wanted leading to our pretty little country cottage. Roy and I were both agreed that we would replace it as soon as possible but, after the move and the costs involved, money was tight for a while and so the job got put off. But, finally, we were able to have a beautiful path made – one with bricks that looked instantly aged and that evoked the spirit of a true cottage garden. We even widened the top of the path near the front door so it gave us a sunny corner in which to sit among the pots of plants I placed there. It soon became a favourite spot both of ours and of Hattie's. A place to watch the world go by, to listen to the bees in the lavender and inhale the scent of the roses. It would be another thing that we would miss when we left.

There was so much of us in this garden. Not just the toil and the sweat – the hours we'd laboured – but our hearts and our minds, the things we'd chosen to grow, the plants we'd loved and nurtured. We had planted a second mulberry tree, a damson and a pear tree, several elderberries and a lovely hedge full of hawthorn and other native British species, and there was another hedge of rugosa roses whose flowers in the summer and hips in the autumn were so very beautiful.

The garden was us in plant form and it would be hard to give it up, to hand it over to strangers who may very well have their own ideas, and rightly so. I remember one of the cottages we viewed when we were moving from London to Suffolk. It had had the prettiest cottage garden to the front. Alas the cottage was too small for us, but I often thought of it and, one day, we found ourselves driving up that way and couldn't resist having a little peep at it. It had sold and the new owners had ripped out the front garden and had gravelled it over so that they could park two large cars on it and place their wheelie bins at the front. It was a practical use of the space, one cannot disagree with that, but it seemed so very heartless, and rather pointless to buy such a pretty place and then do that to it.

But weren't we already planning what we would do when we moved into Old Thatch? In my mind, I had already dug up half the lawn and had installed raised beds and flower borders. What would the current owners think of that? Perhaps they loved the large lawned areas. Maybe, to their minds, open space was easy to manage and beautiful to look at and I was just making a lot of work for myself. Houses and gardens have to work for the owners and it's their right to put their mark upon a place and make it truly theirs.

Village Life… and Death

Although I'd grown up in small villages in rural Norfolk, I'd never stayed in one place long enough to really get close to the community. My parents had always loved to move and so we weren't in a property longer than five or six years. This made it hard to put roots down and get to really know people.

Then, when Roy and I were living in London, although we were there for eleven years and surrounded by many people, we didn't really get to know any of them apart from our immediate neighbours. There's something about the terraced houses of the London suburbs that kind of prevents getting emotionally close to your neighbours even though you are in close physical proximity to them.

So when we moved to our little village in Suffolk, we really weren't prepared for the friends we would make there. We had heard all sorts of horror stories about how hard it was to blend into village life and be welcomed. The old joke was that you had to be at least fifth-generation to be accepted. The thought was terrifying. After all, we were coming from London and, even though I'd been brought up in East Anglia, that might not be good enough. But we needn't have worried because we were made so welcome and the people we got to know soon became good friends.

In the nine years that we were in the village, we sadly lost three friends, but there was one that hit us particularly hard. Annie was one of the first people to call on us when we moved into Mulberry Cottage, inviting us to her home and introducing us to her own friends. It was such a lovely gesture to reach out to us like that and introduce us to others. We felt instantly welcomed and cared about.

Over the years, our friendship grew. We looked after Annie and her husband's home on many occasions, taking care of the chickens and their two mischievous cats. I joined the village walking group and I remember one walk in particular because I was struggling to cross a field that had recently been ploughed. The ridges had deep trenches either side of them and I was wobbling all over the place. If there's one thing that terrifies me, it's losing my balance and I was beginning to panic. Cue Annie who walked alongside me and let me lean on her. We must have made a funny sight because she was so much smaller than I was. Smaller but stronger.

Then there was the time she and her husband booked the Grayson Perry house to stay in and invited Roy and I to join them. Called 'A House for Essex', it's situated near Wrabness overlooking the River Stour with extensive views towards the port at Felixstowe.

More than just a house, this is a work of art with giant tapestries depicting the life of Julie Cope – a mythical Essex woman created by Perry. Inspired by architectural traditions of chapels and memorials, it's built in four sections of increasing height. It's clad in two thousand handmade tiles in a bottle green with a shine like enamel, and is topped with a golden roof. Inside, it's a feast for the eyes and the mind, for each piece tells us a little bit about his character, Julie, including the impressive motorbike

hanging from the ceiling of the main room which, in the story of Julie's life, knocked her down and killed her.

Waking up in a room with one of Grayson Perry's enormous tapestries in their vivid colours towering above me was an experience that only comes once in a lifetime. It was such a unique and remarkable building and it was typical of Annie and her husband to want to share that experience with friends.

I shared so many wonderful moments with Annie. We used to go swimming together each week and one trip I particularly remember is when she struck up a conversation with somebody while in the steam room. I'm a little shy around strangers and tend not to chat easily, but Annie wasn't like that at all. She always wanted to get to know people. She wanted to find out how they ticked, what they did for a living, and what they had in common with her or not.

Losing Annie was so hard. I'll never forget the day when she came round to Mulberry Cottage with her husband to tell us her news. I put the kettle on and she sidled up to me in the kitchen and casually said that she had only a few months left to live. It isn't the kind of thing you expect to hear when counting out teabags. But her cancer of some years before had returned and there was no escaping it this time.

Inspirational to the end, she had a stream of visitors. Not for her was shutting the world out while she slowly slipped away. She wanted to see everyone and spend every minute she could with the people she loved, even inviting me to her home to cook a new recipe with her.

A mutual friend who was writing a speech for her funeral asked if he could come over and read it to us. He was a bag of nerves. He'd never done anything like this before, he told us. Although friendly and outgoing, the thought of addressing the congregation paralysed him. But he needn't have worried. His speech was full of warmth and poignancy and so many humorous moments. In other words, it was filled with the essence of our friend, Annie.

Unsurprisingly, the church was packed for her funeral and her daughters each gave the most moving speeches. I think I was in tears throughout the whole service and, more than three years on, I still miss my friend greatly. She was truly one of a kind.

And that's one of the problems with village life – it's inevitable that you're going to get close to people and it's going to hurt so very much when you lose them.

Preparing to Move

It's a well-known fact that writers have a lot of books. Some writers are appalled by the very idea of parting with a single tome, but I'm not such a writer. There's nothing I love more than a good sort out and I don't believe you should keep everything you've ever owned in perpetuity. The homes I have lived in haven't been big enough to allow that. But I do think that, even if I lived in a mansion, I'd still have a book cull every so often. After all, I am discovering and buying new books all the time and I like to make room for the latest arrivals.

Ahead of our move, I walk around our home. I note that I have nine bookcases. I don't dare count the number of books in each one, but one bookcase alone holds over one hundred and fifty titles. I also have a very special bookcase on our landing which is home to only one author: Miss Read. Her first novel, *Village School*, was published in 1955 and her final novel, *A Peaceful Retirement*, in 1996. I have almost every title she ever wrote including her children's books, cook book and memoirs, and there are many duplicates because I have both the hardback and paperback editions of each of her country-set novels in the Fairacre and Thrush Green series and even a few signed ones. You could say I'm a bit of a fan.

I also have a lot of research books, and each novel I write usually means buying more books in the way of research. For example, when I was researching Jane Austen for my Austen Addicts series, I bought half a dozen reference books. Was I ever likely to read those again? Probably not. I also believe in letting things go once you have used them. It seems silly to me to hold onto something that I'm no longer going to use when somebody else might get some pleasure from it. I also like the feeling of exchange: as I let one book go, another may find its way to me and I will have room for it in my home.

Authors are always being sent books to read and review or as part of our agreement with our publisher. When each new book of mine is published, my publisher sends a box of paperbacks and audio books to me, as well as several copies of each foreign edition. If an author were to keep all the books that came their way, they would soon be buried under the sheer mass.

For me, it's always a joy to give books away to friends. My lovely farmer friend, who we now consider family since our egg and hen exchange, lives at the end of a long bumpy track and it's always a thrill to leave a little book parcel for her in the metal post box at the beginning of the track. Special Book Delivery, I call it, dropping her an email to let her know it's there.

Following my latest sort out, I also deliver bags and bags of books to the local charity shops and even pop a few on the wall at the front of our cottage – free to anyone who fancies them. They prove very popular.

While it's wonderfully comforting to be surrounded by books and to always have something to read, it can also be a little overwhelming and I soon realise that trimming down my collection allows me to focus on the titles that I do keep. I'm soon rediscovering books I bought years ago but have never read: beautiful vintage hardbacks like a signed copy of an H E Bates autobiography that I treated myself to and an old first edition of a Daphne du Maurier collection of short stories. It's wonderful to find them as if for the first time and I determine to read them, to give them the time that they deserve.

Moving house really makes you think about your possessions and I quickly realise that I am now accountable for decades' worth of collecting and keeping hold of things that really don't have a place in my life anymore. Their time with me is done; I do not need them. They have journeyed with me this far, but our relationship is now over. There's also the fact that, if I keep them, I will have to clean and pack them, unpack them and clean them, find a home for them and also pay for the carriage, and why would I do that with hundreds of items that I no longer love?

As I sort out, I continue to find some dear old friends I haven't paid enough attention to over the years. There's a delicious old hardback about herbs and spices and I'm instantly transported back to the day I bought it. I must have been a student and obviously didn't have a lot of money so a hardback book was a bit of a luxury. But I remember seeing it on the shelf in the little bookshop that used to be housed in the buttery of Carlisle Cathedral. I took it down, holding its great weight in my hands. I didn't know anything about herbs and spices. My family didn't grow them or use them in cooking. We didn't even use pepper. In our family home during the seventies and eighties, salt was the only thing we ever added to our food, but I was nevertheless drawn to these exotic foods. Perhaps the future me was sending a message back in time saying, 'You'll need this one day'.

I also can't help giving some of my attention to the slimmest volume I find. It's *The Snow Goose* by Paul Gallico. I remember it as one of the books we read at school and, although I don't remember the names of the two characters or even that it's set in the neighbouring county of Essex, I remember the *feel* of the book: the cold, wintry marshes, the isolation of the hero and the goodness of his heart. It's not even forty pages long, but it has left its mark on me and I read it again with all the sense of wonder and joy as that first time when I read it as a young schoolgirl.

Then there's J B Priestley's play, *An Inspector Calls* – so clever and captivating, but years of teaching it to pupils means I'll never want to read it for pleasure again. It's the same with Shakespeare – having been thoroughly spoilt studying so many at university and then having the great honour of seeing many performances at The Globe Theatre while living in London, I feel quite sated, so I take my copies of *The Taming of the Shrew*, *Macbeth* and *Romeo and Juliet* to the charity shops.

It's then that I find some ravishing picture books on cottage gardens and cottage interiors on my shelves and I have to take a moment to flip through them, staring at the photos and thinking about our own future home, gazing longingly at flower-choked borders and wood-panelled rooms. Of course, this is a terrible interruption to the business of sorting out and I soon return them to the shelf. I'm meant to be sorting not dreaming.

It's funny the way books can transport you back in time to when you first bought or read them. Within their pages, you can reconnect with your younger self while seeing them with new eyes because you have changed. That's the great gift of a book – you can read them over and over again, finding new things you didn't spot before or rediscovering wonderful passages. Scenes in a novel will resonate differently with you because you are now a different person and you're bringing all your life experience to the story you're reading. That's what keeps so many books on my shelves now – ones I can never part with because they are a true part of me.

Other than my vast book collection, another thing I quickly learned to let go of for this move was photographs. I have a big wooden chest in my study and it has been full of photo albums for decades and I have to say that I rarely look at them. I adore photographs. There's nothing lovelier than a beautiful image framed in silver placed in special corner of your home, but these albums were neglected, unseen and unloved and it was time I went through them. Listening to a series of podcasts on minimalism to keep me company, I was ruthless, pulling out generic photos of landscapes that I'd loved, people I'd once worked with but whose names I could no longer remember, and blurred images of pets from the past. By the end, I had around a dozen empty albums destined for the charity shops. Did people even buy albums anymore, I wondered? Or had digital replaced the need for them? It does seem a shame to me that so much has gone digital. I know I have lost countless photos on my computer because I just can't remember where I have filed them. And digital technology encourages us to take so many more. But it really felt good to let go of some of the images that just didn't have a place in my life anymore.

Papers were next. I have so much paperwork. Whenever I start a novel, I bring out an A4 folder and stuff it full of notes, photos, postcards and maps – anything that might help me to enter the new world of my novel. After having written more than thirty books, I have quite a few of these and I begin going through them now, ruthlessly tearing out anything that is no longer needed. This results in a stack of folders and plastic wallets which I can't bear to put in the bin for landfill. Luckily, I find a friend who is now working from home and who is happy to have some free stationery. And that's part of the great joy of a good sort out – what you no longer need, somebody else might.

The Law of Attraction

I'm not a terribly superstitious person, but I do love discovering the different ways people think, and different belief systems. As a storyteller, these always fascinate me and I often find myself reading up on a subject that I might not believe in personally, but which is nevertheless interesting. When I heard about The Law of Attraction, it captured my imagination.

A couple of years ago, I started house-sitting on a regular basis. I'd done it for friends and had always enjoyed having a change of scene and taking care of somebody else's beloved pets. One place I house-sat, during a cold spring week, was a beautiful pink farmhouse with extensive gardens. I was taking care of two Jack Russell terriers and the world's friendliest cat. The animals were so loving and it was a complete pleasure to look after them. One thing I enjoyed was to sit out in the garden, fussing the older dog who couldn't walk very far but still enjoyed a tootle around the garden and a roll in the grass while his belly was being rubbed. I took a few funny selfies one morning of the two of us sitting on the lawn with the house behind us and it wasn't until I got home that I realised the house was the spitting image of a little photograph I had pinned on the notice board above my desk. I had torn it out of a magazine, dreaming about a time when I might write about such a beautiful place or even be lucky to own something like it. Well, I haven't yet taken ownership of such a place, but I kind of had for that one week, hadn't I? Had I made that happen myself, I wondered? Had I been looking at that picture for so long that it had become a part of me and I'd attracted it towards me via the house-sitting site I'd joined? Thinking about that gave me great pleasure and a lot of food for thought.

Although I'm married to an artist, I'm not at all artistic myself, other than my writing. At school, I struggled with drawing and painting although it was something I enjoyed. I was much happier with a ball of clay, making mythical creatures that didn't resemble anything in particular. But I remember that I used to have one drawing I would repeat over and over again and it was of a country cottage. I don't know where this image came from but it was always the same: it had a thatched roof, two dormer windows upstairs, two casement windows downstairs and an arched front door in the centre. Of course, roses grew around the door, and there was a curved path leading to a little gate at the front of the property. I had never lived in a thatched cottage growing up. The oldest property I'd lived in was Edwardian. So I can't quite remember where this dream of a thatched cottage came from. Living in villages in rural Norfolk, we had our fair share of pretty homes, but I certainly never came across one that looked like this.

And then Pink Thatch came into my life.

Roy and I love the Open Studios here in Suffolk. Every June, artists across the county open their studios to members of the public and you can visit as many as you like. I'm always very excited when I pick up the brochure, turning the pages, looking at the artwork produced by these talented people and planning visits around them, but I have a confession. I'm not just looking at the art. I do also look at where the studio is. So, for example, if the artist lives on Station Road in the centre of a town, I am much less likely to visit than if the address were Church Lane in a rural village. I'm a country girl at heart and there's nothing I love more than visiting country homes.

One year, the directions to the artist's studio mentioned a pink thatched cottage. That was all I needed. I circled the name of the artist and we visited that weekend. The cottage was tucked away down a track in a remote village and was storybook perfect with its pretty garden full of blue delphiniums and pink roses. And the artist was lovely too. There are some people in life you instantly connect with and she was one of those people. Perhaps it was because we had friends in common, but I think it was more than that. We liked the same things. *Loved* the same things.

'Would you like to see the garden?' she asked us after we'd looked at her beautiful pastels and collages in colours that made the heart sing.

'Yes please!' we said.

She showed us round the vegetable garden where heaps of salad grew alongside flowers she'd cut to paint. She took us into the orchard and then out into a large meadow, its long grasses waving in the summer breeze. I was in heaven.

'I don't suppose you'd like to house-sit the cottage while we're away?' she suddenly asked.

I did a double take. It was as though she was reading from a script I had written in my imagination.

'I'd love to!' I told her, not really believing that this was going to happen, but hoping so much that it would.

For three weeks that summer, I found myself living at Pink Thatch. To have so much space and beauty around me was a welcome relief from the recent stresses of our own village which was getting progressively noisier. This was a real treat.

The owner's purpose-built studio in the garden was light and airy and I made myself a standing desk at one of her workbenches on which I placed my laptop, opening the doors in front and to the side of the studio so that I could hear birdsong as I worked.

I cooked simple meals in the Aga, picking a few salad leaves each day from the vegetable garden which it was my job to keep watered that summer, and I went to bed a lot earlier than I do at home, getting up earlier too to enjoy the warm summer mornings.

There's a special freedom that comes from staying in a place that isn't yours. You don't worry about things in the same way you do at home. All those little jobs you should be doing like repairs or decorating. You don't have to open the bills that arrive and you don't even have to answer the telephone. It's incredibly liberating and it allows the mind to wander, giving you the sort of space that normal life denies you.

We went back to Pink Thatch just before putting Mulberry Cottage on the market. It was just as lovely as I'd remembered from the previous summer, with the roses, delphiniums and dahlias in bloom in the front garden, and with the happy addition of some chickens and a marvellous polytunnel full of produce. We must remember this, we said to each other. This feeling of peace and space. We can't compromise when we move. We must have a beautiful garden, a beautiful home.

But we weren't looking for a thatched cottage at that stage. We were not looking for something that was timber-framed with casement windows and no double glazing. And yet, the more I thought about it, the more I remembered those glorious feelings of serenity I had experienced at Pink Thatch. Then I remembered that funny little picture I used to draw as a child. The thatched cottage with dormer windows. Had I made this happen? It would be very easy to believe that I had and that my dreams had manifested a home for us.

Last Summer at Mulberry Cottage

We had a heatwave in May and we realised how very lucky we were to have our garden and it was heaven to sit outside in the sunshine, a stack of good books to read. I kicked off my shoes and wriggled my feet in the grass. This isn't as blissful as it sounds for the grass is kept extraordinarily short by the hens and the rabbits, and you take your life in your hands going barefoot when you have a flock of hens. But, after our long British winter, it felt good to spend time outdoors.

As a writer, I tend to spend a lot of time inside, hunched over my keyboard, and a rather lovely treat for me is to accompany Roy on one of his painting trips which, during our last summer at Mulberry Cottage, involved painting a lot of stooks – a favourite subject matter of his. A stook – or shock as it's also called in Suffolk – is a group of sheaves of grain which are stood up in the field so that the head of the grain is away from the ground, prior to collecting for threshing and using for thatching. They are very picturesque – more so than the commonplace haystack although we have a lot of round hay and straw stacks in the Stour Valley and they can look very lovely too.

A few years ago, Roy got to know a local thatcher and now wanted to ask his permission to paint in the fields he was harvesting this year. It isn't hard to find him in the local fields and, one evening at dusk, we park our car and cross a field to say hello. The field is stubble now, the stooks in the process of being stacked. We spend a pleasant few minutes chatting to him as the moon rises in the trees behind us and we hear the hooting of a nearby owl. It feels slightly illicit to be in this place so late. Nature is claiming it and we have no place there, it seems to be telling us.

We tell the thatcher about the house we are hoping to buy and he says he knows it well. He probably knows all the thatched properties in the area but, alas, this is one he hasn't worked on. He tells us when it was last thatched and I'm amazed that he knows the date so readily. This is good news for us as it means it has many more years of life in it. We chat some more and Roy is given permission to paint in the field and the adjoining one too where there are even more stooks.

It's lovely to see an old tradition like this alive and well. There is something so earthy and real about gathering plants in order to make a roof for one's home. It really connects you to the landscape around you.

New Viewings

After losing our initial buyers at the end of August, Mulberry Cottage goes back onto the market. Of course, when the viewings start up again, the hens are in the middle of a huge moult. Perdita is the first to begin, shedding her paisley patterned feathers all over the garden, and looking like a little ragbag of a hen instead of the glorious duchess that she truly is. Then, Phoebe joins her. Phoebe is our Black Orpington and begins to shed her dark feathers with their flash of iridescent green right across the lawn. We think it's rather beautiful and amusing, but what will viewers think? I don't want to get the chance to find out so I spend a good deal of each morning picking feathers off the lawn.

Chickens do not look good when they're moulting and Phoebe looks particularly scrawny around the neck with most of her feathers missing from there. It's hard not to laugh, but one really shouldn't mock a moulting hen; one should have every sympathy with them because it really must be an awful thing to go through.

As the time between viewings stretched and we weren't getting any offers, paranoia began to set in. Were we the only people who could ever love Mulberry Cottage? Could nobody else see its beauty?

One of the viewings seemed to go particularly well, but the viewer says he won't put an offer in until he has a buyer for his place. This is frustrating because our sellers have found a property they want, but the seller of that won't accept their offer until we have a buyer for ours so, for a while, we appear to be stuck.

Finally, a call comes through from the estate agent. We have an offer. A very cheeky offer, he tells us, relating the figure. Our hearts plummet. It's not the full asking price as it was with our initial buyers, but they've gone and this is what we have now. We turn it down and the negotiations begin. Two long days of phone calls ensue and we have a sale at the end of it. It's not quite what we were hoping for, but we don't want to lose Old Thatch and we don't want to be trying to sell a house as autumn and winter kick in.

It appears that we're in a chain of six and that there's a woman renting at the end of it. This seems doable. We are moving closer to making Old Thatch ours. But I'm so anxious. I'm not normally an anxious person, but I really want this to work – I *need* it to work – and it's never fun being needy. And so I throw myself into my work, challenging myself to write as much as I can before the house move because I know I'll want to give myself some time off to enjoy organising our new home.

Our Audrey

One morning in October, I'm in the garden seeing to the hens when I hear an odd noise coming from the nest boxes. I open the door and Portia is in the far nest box on egg laying duty, but it's Audrey, our young white hen, who is making a noise like we've never heard before in ten years of hen-keeping. She's standing up, squawking, and is obviously in distress. As she moves out of the nest box, I see a yolky mess on her white feathers underneath her vent. An egg has broken inside her.

This is something I've been dreading. A few months before, Audrey wasn't well. She was standing around looking despondent, her wings lowered, which is always a bad sign. I have a little saying: a still hen is an ill hen. Hens rarely just stand still during daylight hours. They're either bathing or preening or hunting for food. When they just stand around – particularly if they hide behind or underneath things – it's time to make a call to the vets.

We never really discovered what was wrong with her that first time, but she pretty much stopped laying eggs afterwards, producing the occasional tiny egg or soft-shelled one. It wasn't a good sign and we'd been keeping an eye on her ever since. So, on that October morning, I rush her inside, attempting to give her a warm bath to ease things, but she really isn't happy about being dunked in water. Roy rings the vets and we pop Audrey into a box to travel into town. I stay at home to walk Hattie. I usually always go with my hens, but the Covid-19 regulations mean that vet consultations are taking place in the car park and you can't accompany your pet inside.

I walk Hattie, trying to think positive thoughts. She's a young hen, I tell myself. Young and strong. And she made a recovery last time. She can do that again, can't she?

Alas, when we get back home, the phone rings and it's Roy. He's sitting in the car having just spoken to the vet and the news isn't good. Audrey is not in good shape and recovery is unlikely. She has egg yolk peritonitis and there are complications. She's in distress and the kindest thing we can do is to put her to sleep. I agree with tears streaming down my face at the knowledge I won't see my beautiful pale girl again, and with the pain that I'm not there with her, holding her as she slips away.

I worry that Mini P will suffer from the loss of her sister and friend. Hens do tend to have a companion and these two, being hatched at the same time and being a whole year younger than the other three in our flock, were natural friends. But I needn't have worried. She seems quite happy. Animals, on the whole, accept the present and just get on with things and, although this may seem heartless to us, it is a blessing. But our little flock isn't the same without Audrey. It feels so much smaller and I miss seeing her cheeky little face peeping in to the conservatory from the top of the bench she loved to jump onto.

The In-between Time

It's always astonishing to me how many bits of paper you need in order to move house and how long the whole process takes. It's a long enough process even if things go smoothly, but throw a few problems in and it can take an absolute age.

One important document we had to sign hadn't got the right information on it and had to be redrafted. This happened twice. Had we not noticed, we would have sold Mulberry Cottage without its beautiful meadow. Now, we wouldn't have minded keeping the meadow, but that really wouldn't have been fair on the buyers, would it?

In the months leading up to the move, I'm horribly restless. I find it difficult to commit to anything and I flit from reading one book to another, putting each down in turn, unsatisfied, looking for something more. My writing is the same. It's bitty and doesn't give me the contentedness that it usually does. I'm normally a one thousand words a day kind of writer but, during this time, I'm lucky if I limp to five hundred, and I'm all over the place with it, writing out of sequence and struggling to connect scenes.

I suppose that, once you know a new life is around the corner, you want to start living it as soon as possible and anything else feels unsatisfactory. I'm living in a kind of twilight world, an in-between stage where I'm no longer at Mulberry Cottage but nor am I at Old Thatch.

I go from room to room, wondering if I've perhaps missed a drawer or a cupboard that needs to be rooted through and sorted out before we move, but it seems like I've done most of them. Roy orders boxes so that he can pack his artist's studio up ahead of the removal men arriving. It's a huge task. He's been collecting his artist's materials there for over nine years and there are many large canvases and frames, all of which are delicate and which Roy wants to be in charge of packing himself.

As we slowly make some progress with our packing, taking books from shelves and paintings from the walls, I start wondering how much art Roy and I have created in our time at Mulberry Cottage. I do a quick bit of addition and soon discover that I've written thirteen novels here – ten published and three, at the time of writing this, unpublished. I've also written nine novellas including five Christmas stories, three memoirs – my Mulberry Cottage collection – and one screenplay. That's a decent number of words, I think. But how many paintings has Roy painted? It's impossible to say, but it will be in the high hundreds. He doesn't keep them all – some are sold, some get painted over and some, after being kept for a lengthy period, get scrapped. One thing is certain, though: Mulberry Cottage and the countryside surrounding it has been a rich source of inspiration to us both and we are no doubt leaving a little bit of us and our art behind when we leave.

At last, an email arrives from our solicitor saying that our buyers are ready to exchange and a proposed completion date is given for the middle of February. That's just over a month away now. Suddenly, it all seems very real – as if all the hurdles have been leapt over at last and we can finally start planning our new life.

The removal company delivers the boxes while I'm out walking Hattie. Roy is standing in a narrow strip in the middle of the dining room when I return because that is the only space left. Everywhere else is covered in flat boxes. It's a little overwhelming. They fill the doorways, cover radiators and balance against tables. The air is filled with the scent of them. Some are new and white – for books and crockery, we've been told. Others are brown and older – they've been used before and have amusing notes on from previous moves. *Pasta and spices*, we read on one. *Games room* on another. We've also been given rolls of thick tape with which to make the boxes up. We take a deep breath and make a start.

Even after my huge sort out of the summer, there is still so much to pack. Where does it all come from? How can two people accumulate so much stuff? Do we really need it all? Just glassware alone fills several cupboards.

It isn't until we've packed all but the essentials that I take a step back and examine what's left. These are the few personal pieces that have remained unpacked until the last possible moment. There's a notebook and pencil, a woollen blanket, a lip balm, a pair of reading glasses, a paperback and an e-reader and a couple of my favourite crystals. It is me in essence, and it does make me wonder how much of the other stuff I really need.

Last Days at Mulberry Cottage

It's the day before we're meant to be exchanging contracts and news comes from our estate agent that the woman at the bottom of the chain in rented accommodation has had to extend her lease owing to the number of delays. Now, she is struggling and will have to find somewhere else to rent which means more expense for her. She is panicking and this makes us panic. She's threatening to pull out and collapse the whole chain. I can't bear it. The thought of having to start all over again if our buyer's buyer does this. Not only will it cost us time, but we could potentially lose Old Thatch and that would mean starting again with a house search, costing us not only all the money we've paid to our solicitor but the full structural survey we had done on the property. And there's also the stamp duty to consider. The government's stamp duty holiday is due to finish at the end of March. If we miss this deadline, it will cost us an extra £15,000.

Roy makes a decision – we will offer the woman renting a few hundred pounds to help her with her expenses. We put it to the estate agent and the owners of Old Thatch and our buyers agree to offer the same. We then wait. Finally, she comes back – she wants ten times what we offered. We are astounded. She is not the only one with extra costs. The delays have cost everybody in the chain. We've all got our own worries, and us reaching out to her was something we didn't have to do at all, but she knows she's the one in control and that she can collapse the whole chain. We tell our estate agent how we feel and he's in agreement. We won't give her what she wants, but we'll stand by the original sum we offered. The message is passed back.

Word comes up the chain that we are finally ready to exchange contracts and then we discover that our solicitor has gone on holiday without telling us and there is nobody else is in the office who can handle the exchange. If we miss it, our booking with our removal company and that of everybody else's will be lost again. Roy gets on the phone.

Finally, an emergency call is put out at our solicitor's company and a replacement is found, only she's due to have her Covid jab on the day of exchange. 'But don't worry. I'll take your file with me,' she assures us.

And so it's done – her vaccination and our exchange of contracts – weeks after we were initially meant to exchange and after having lost our removal company twice. We can now make plans for completion as there is a firm date in the diary.

With the time all this has taken, moving house will now coincide with one of the busiest periods in a gardener's calendar: seed sowing time! I have been calendar watching for weeks now, deliberating whether to start planting before we move, but young seedlings are vulnerable and I'm not sure it's a good idea to transport them when they're so fragile. But, as we're now in the middle of February, I can wait no longer and buy a small propagator for sowing. I choose three kinds of tomato, two kinds of aubergine, some sweet peppers and some chilli peppers which all need to be sown early in order to make the very most of our erratic English summers when hot days are not always guaranteed.

It's not ideal to be sowing seeds in the run-up to moving house but, luckily, we are on good terms with our sellers and they agree to let us deliver my precious cargo and a few other plants to their greenhouse at Old Thatch the day before the actual move.

The house is now full of boxes. The removal company is coming to do a 'fragile pack' for us – taking care of ornaments, glass and china. This removes a huge strain. Checking around the house, I see two paintings which Roy is in the process of packing. They were in my study – beautiful paintings of pink roses and peonies by one of our artist friends, Haidee-Jo Summers. But, as I'm holding them, I trip over a box and drop the two paintings which have been sealed together in bubble wrap. They land, corner down, on my left big toe and I scream in shock and pain. Roy is concerned, but I tease him because I'm not altogether sure if it's concern for me or the paintings which he framed for me in gesso and gold leaf. Sure enough, my toe later sports a huge bruise, looking as if I've dipped it in a bottle of ink. But the paintings survived.

Another last-minute job is going through the freezer. As I do so, it strikes me that we make an awful lot of soup and the trouble is, it's almost always orange – a vague sort of orange that could be squash or sweet potato or carrot or a mixture of all three. It's a fun sort of surprise what you're going to get. We really should label things properly, but I always believe I'll remember exactly what it is I'm squirreling away… until I dig it out again a few months later. 'Surprise Soup' we call it.

There are numerous other things in the depths of the freezer – strange red squares which it takes me a while to identify as the tomato sauce I've prepared in ice cube trays. I vow to be much more organised once we've moved to Old Thatch.

The Day of the Move

The weather report isn't good, but it could be worse. If we'd been moving on the original date suggested to us in February, there would have been three inches of snow on the ground, making it tricky to move or even find our garden furniture and pots. So we count our lucky stars that we simply have a gale blowing.

Last winter's leaves scurry into the house as quickly as our boxes are taken out. Doors are slamming shut, shredding my nerves as I do my best to tidy up and clean as the removal guys do their job. They're great chaps and go above and beyond their allotted duties, helping us to pack last-minute items like the stuff from the loft which we hadn't got around to bringing down until the morning of the move.

Time seems to speed up and it's midday when we run out of it. I want to vacuum the living room, but our buyers' three removal lorries are now parked outside our little cottage, looming ominously. This is no longer your home, they seem to say. It's time to go.

I'd promised myself that I wouldn't get emotional about leaving Mulberry Cottage because it was something I'd chosen to do but, the night before, our neighbours had come round with gifts of lemon cake and a potted rose for our new cottage garden. It was so very kind and sweet, but it was the message they'd written in the card that made me cry – they were thanking us for being such lovely neighbours and telling us we would be missed.

So I'd cried my tears the night before and there isn't time to shed any more as we close the door of Mulberry Cottage, locking it for the last time.

The hens have been popped into a big box with plenty of holes for ventilation. Luckily, hens calm down quickly when they're somewhere fairly dark and they're no bother at all once we get them onto the back seat of the car. However, the car is so packed that there's only one small space for Hattie – in my footwell. She's never travelled like this before – neither have I for that matter – and she objects to getting into the car at all. Roy manages to coax her in and she immediately tries to climb onto my lap and we take off with her half on and half off. It's very uncomfortable and I'm glad our drive is relatively short compared to our London to Suffolk journey of nine years ago.

We have a two hour wait while the removal men at Old Thatch finish their job. We chat with our sellers though their kitchen window. They give us a drink and tell us about some photos and documents they've left for us about the property. We give Hattie a little walk and check on the hens, and then it's time. The money has been transferred and Old Thatch is ours.

The removal men get to work, unloading all that they loaded a few hours ago. They are cheerful and hard-working and we feel just awful when one of the young guys cracks his head – several times – on the low door linking the kitchen and dining room. Does the company warn them about the kind of property they'll be working in that day, I ask? Nope, he replies. They should, I think. There should definitely be some kind of message telling them that they'll be working with low beams and doorframes and to be vigilant!

I ask him what's the worst kind of house move to do and he replies, without hesitation, 'Rich people'. He tells me he hates the big eight-bedroom moves where the people have so much stuff absolutely everywhere and aren't even aware of what they have. It makes me thankful that I've never had more than three bedrooms to fill with my things.

That first night in Old Thatch is very strange. We are aware of every new sound and smell. The weather is wild. The gale is still raging and we're grateful for our warm bed even if it is surrounded by boxes. But what a strange feeling it is. We're suddenly the owners of a very old listed building with countless beams, two inglenook fireplaces, a couple of bread ovens and an Aga.

It's a big responsibility, but we couldn't be happier.

Settling In

There's a lot to get used to at Old Thatch – for a start, there are far more rooms than at Mulberry Cottage. It all seems massive to us although it is still only a three-bedroomed house. But the rooms themselves are bigger especially the kitchen. Actually, it's the kitchen I'm most excited about. It's my idea of heaven – a big square room with a royal blue Aga at its heart. Our last kitchen was galley style and you could touch both walls on either side at the same time. If Roy and I were in it together, you could guarantee a slight conflict of interests, and there was no workspace either. The one tiny area where we prepped food and baked was less than a metre long between the sink and the cooker's hob. So this new kitchen is a wonder to me and I marvel that you have to physically walk across it to reach cupboards rather than simply turning around as we did at Mulberry Cottage. I envisage myself spending far more time cooking and baking, bottling and stewing. There is room to spread out here, to relax into a cooking project, and the Aga will make it a cosy hideaway during the cold months of the year.

That first week at Old Thatch is busy not only with unpacking and cleaning cupboards and deciding where everything should go, but with sowing seeds too. Spring means that I spend a good deal of my time out in the garden and, to be honest, it's nice to get away from unpacking boxes for a bit and dream about the

garden. I bring out my three seed tins, wondering why I felt the need to order even more seeds over the winter when there are still so many packets in the tins. But it's an annual treat I cannot deny myself and it's always fun to try and grow new varieties each year as well as old favourites. One year, the new plant I decided to grow was cucamelon – a curious little fruit not much bigger than your thumbnail, with a fabulous crunch and a taste like something between a cucumber and melon. Another year, it was celeriac – an odd-looking plant – half football, half alien. That's the thing with seed catalogues – they're so very tempting with their photographs and delicious descriptions. It's hard to pass anything by, but I sternly remind myself each and every year that I don't have to grow absolutely everything in one season. So I narrow my choices down with a reluctant sigh.

The seeds I planted in the run-up to the move are doing well and I now sow some cosmos and zinnias, salad and cucumbers. I've never grown cucumbers before as our greenhouse at Mulberry Cottage was a little small, but there is far more space here and I'm feeling ambitious. I am going to scale everything up this year.

The weather is still bitterly cold, but there is evidence of spring all around the garden with delightfully bright primroses opening in the borders and daffodils under the ancient apple tree. This apple tree, standing in the middle of the lawn in the south part of the garden, is a real beauty. Its trunk is wider than I am and is gnarled and mossy, its branches almost equally thick. I wonder how old it is. It will certainly have stood witness to many of the owners who have come and gone over the years.

As I enjoy the garden, I remember a quote I love from Helen Thomas who was the wife of the poet Edward Thomas: 'There's nothing left to wish for – we are in the country and it is spring.' I am inclined to agree. But there's a lot to do. For a start, there are only two small raised beds in the garden – not enough for the food I want to grow in the coming seasons. So we order two tonnes of top soil and compost to be delivered. It arrives in massive sacks which have to be lifted off the lorry by crane. It's really something to watch and we become slightly anxious that we've ordered far too much and that we won't be able to move it all ourselves. Still, better to have too much than too little, I reason, and we'll get fit with our efforts with the wheelbarrow.

We are going to try making beds using the no-dig method. We've never done this before, but we're up for the challenge and we believe it will be quicker, cheaper and easier in the first year than creating raised beds. For one thing, it saves a lot of digging. We can also recycle some of the boxes we have from moving house, placing them straight onto the ground and giving them a good soak before covering them in top soil and compost. The cardboard acts as a weed suppressant, killing off anything nasty as well as the grass that isn't needed. We have a lot of lawn here at Old Thatch and don't mind sacrificing a bit in order to grow produce. But I do worry that the edges won't be as neat as having raised beds. We invested in these at Mulberry Cottage and they looked wonderful – for a few years. Alas, wood doesn't last well and, after just three years, a lot of it needed replacing. So we'll try this no-dig method and see how we get on.

History

It is wonderful to own a property that has been a dwelling for so long. How many families have lived here? What did they all do? Did they work the land? What did they grow in the garden? How were the fireplaces used? Were the bread ovens used every day? I think it would be fun to see if we can find any records.

One of the photos that the previous owners left us is an aerial view of the cottage and you can see that part of the front garden was used to grow vegetables. This is something I'd like to reintroduce. After all, this is how cottage gardens would originally have been used. They were practical places and every inch of soil had to be productive.

Historic England's website describes our cottage as being a timber-framed and plastered building with one storey and attics which is interesting. So that means Roy and I will be working in the attics as that's where our studies are to be. I love that the cottage has gabled dormers and casement windows. They are the very stuff of romance and I often write about such architectural gems in my novels, but I've never had the pleasure of owning anything like this before.

When we received the building survey, we got quite a surprise. The surveyor believed the house dates back to 1500. That's one hundred years older than we'd been led to believe. It's the time of the Tudors – when Henry VIII was king and busy getting through his six wives. It was when Michelangelo was painting the Sistine Chapel. It makes me feel I should plant a knot garden or an apothecary's herb garden. There are already many wonderful herbs growing by the back door at Old Thatch, handy for the kitchen, but maybe I should make another herb garden or potager even. The idea excites me.

When we bought Mulberry Cottage, it was the oldest property either of us had ever lived in, built in the early nineteenth-century. That's around the time Jane Austen was publishing all of her wonderful novels. But, with Old Thatch, we travel back to the sixteenth and seventeenth-centuries to when William Shakespeare was penning his great works.

The original, oldest part of the house is believed to have been an open hall house, extended in the sixteenth-century when the addition of a chimney allowed for the construction of an upper floor. A hall house was a simple construction with no fireplace. The fire would have burned in the centre. There are half round pole rafters which the surveyor found to be smoke-blackened – a good indication of the date of the structure. Smoke blackening usually indicates that the property was first built as an open hall with smoke percolating up through the roof via vents.

Most of the half-timbered cottages we see today were built between 1550 and 1650. There was a big boom in building during the reign of Elizabeth I both in terms of grand manor houses – with her subjects outdoing one another and often bankrupting themselves in order to impress their queen – and more humble dwellings. After this date, buildings tended to be added to or altered and this is definitely something that's happened to Old Thatch with later additions being made to the original structure.

Something else the survey shows is evidence of 'roof spread' which is the natural tendency for a roof such as ours to splay outwards at the eaves. We're told it's likely to be old movement and the original structure has now been significantly stiffened and strengthened by the new softwood framework built within the attic area. This is comforting to know.

The report shows us that there are some areas needing attention as one would expect. Just like us, old buildings need to be able to breathe and they suffer if they're covered up especially by the modern materials so many of us have inflicted upon them like the dreaded cement. We will need to assess some of the paintwork especially in the living room where we can see there is a problem. The paintwork there looks as if it's bubbling and will need to come off as it obviously isn't breathable. We want to get things right both for us and the building and, as tempting as it is to get to work with a paintbrush, choosing the colours we want, we know it's going to be more complicated than that and take a little longer.

The living room is a particular light-filled delight to us with two windows facing east, one facing west and one south. The room is divided by a stud wall which would have been the original outside wall of the property. Now, it's been extended and a delightful 'hip roof' can be seen, giving the property a fairytale look with its gently sloping and rounded appearance.

We place Hattie's chair by the south window and she seems very happy with this decision, enjoying the view of the garden from her very own casement window.

I decide that two of my bookcases will live in this part of the living room. There might even be room for another sofa or a comfy armchair too. It's not really a large enough space to call a library, but perhaps it can be a book nook. A cosy place to reach for a book and sit with it by one of the windows enveloped by wisteria in the summer, or snuggled up next to the fire in the winter.

A Brief Bit About Thatch

Thatched properties today seem like an extravagance. They're beautiful, but they're known to be expensive to maintain which is curious as the reason thatch was originally used was because reed and straw were cheap. Some of the earliest homes were made from wattle and daub and roofed with thatch, with all these materials being easily available. One of the reasons it's so expensive now is that special varieties of wheat have to be grown and then harvested using a labour-intensive method to make sure the straw stalks remain long and unbroken.

Reed from Norfolk still makes thatch a popular choice in the counties of East Anglia. And there are many thatched properties in the south and the west country. Hampshire, Dorset, Devon, Somerset, and the Cotswolds boast many beautiful thatched properties. In fact, it's estimated that there are sixty-thousand thatched houses in the UK and seventy-five percent of these are listed.

In the past, when thatch was cheaper, far more buildings were made using it. Corn ricks for housing grain, milk stands by the roadside, canopies to protect notice boards outside village churches or halls, garden sheds and even farm boundary walls. Luckily, here in East Anglia, there are still many thatched pubs and several beautiful churches with thatched roofs.

As well as straw or reed, a thatcher will need a good supply of thatching spars which are made from hazel. These are used to fix the thatch onto the roof. Hundreds will be used in the construction of a roof. There are also shorter lengths of hazel used known as liggers. These are easily visible on the ridges and, in long straw roofs, on the eaves and gable ends too. They can be wonderfully decorative with patterns made between them using small crossed hazel rods called slats.

The thatch just beneath a chimney is also often given special attention. Ours is a beautiful shape of three scallops. These chimney decorations are known as aprons and, along with the ridge pattern, are often a mark of individual thatchers who adopt a style that's their own. Points or scallops are often used right along a ridge, some in alternating patterns. It's become a bit of a hobby of ours now to note these whenever we drive by a thatched property. Some thatchers will even make a decoration for the roof depicting an animal like a rabbit, cat or pheasant, standing proud above the ridge. Some homes even sport witches.

Windows can also look extremely attractive with thatch. We have three dormer windows upstairs with pointed thatched 'eyebrows'. They give the cottage so much character.

Thatched roofs tend to be steeply pitched so that rainwater and snow can shed from them quickly. This works well on narrow houses which are only one room deep as ours is.

I've always adored thatched cottages and have photographed more than my share of them in the past but, buying Old Thatch, I have a renewed interest in them now and buy several books, determining to learn more about this wonderful tradition.

Famous Thatches

There's something special about a thatched cottage. It speaks to us of the past, of simpler times, perhaps, when our homes weren't wired up to the rest of the world twenty-four hours a day and when gardens were integral to living in the country, providing much of the food for the families living in them.

Thomas Hardy's famous birthplace, now owned by the National Trust, is a thatched cottage at Lower Bockhampton in Dorset. It's an iconic country cottage set deep in woodland with the perfect garden full of flowers and herbs surrounding it. I first visited while studying Hardy's novels at university. A friend and I took a trip down there, staying at youth hostels and hiking between Hardy locations, and one clear memory stays with me: spending a moment alone in the room Hardy was born in, taking a second to drink in the scene from the window.

There's another beautiful thatched property in Dorset which is special to me: Woodsford Castle. Built in the fourteenth-century and owned by the Landmark Trust, my husband and I stayed there one summer and what a treat that was. It's an enormous property and boasts one of the largest thatched roofs in the country although it probably wasn't originally thatched as this would have made it too vulnerable to attack. We shared the experience of staying there with some artist and writer friends, eating in the large kitchen on the first floor and swapping stories in the huge great hall. Woodsford's setting is rural and peaceful, a stone's throw from some stunning walks along the Frome – a beautiful chalk stream which winds through the sort of valleys you can imagine Tess Durbeyfield milking cows in.

One very famous thatched property belonged to Shakespeare's wife, Anne Hathaway. This is the quintessential English cottage with its neat thatch, tiny casement windows and perfect cottage garden planting, and it's featured on countless jigsaw puzzles and chocolate boxes.

For many years, children's author, Enid Blyton, lived in a seventeenth-century thatched property at Bourne End, close to the River Thames in Buckinghamshire. It's open to the public and set in delightful gardens where visitors can enjoy tea and cake. Blyton loved the fairytale look of the property and not only wrote many books there, but featured her home in a number of them.

Thatched cottages have always been a popular subject matter for artists, perhaps none more so than Helen Allingham, the Victorian illustrator and watercolourist who painted idyllic scenes of rural life. I adore her paintings and have become newly-obsessed with them now that we own our thatch, flipping through the books I have about her, noticing the tumbledown thatches where slats have come lose and are half-way down the roofs, and where plants clamber ever upwards, threatening to topple chimneys.

Allingham's cottages look as if they have grown out of the countryside with front gardens bursting with summer blooms like foxgloves, hollyhocks and roses. Sunflowers are frequently seen, peeping cheekily over walls and hedges, and this makes me laugh as I am planning on planting some in our own front garden to make passers-by smile.

Her gardens are places the owners take pride in and there is usually somebody outside enjoying the space, whether they're pegging out a line of fresh, white washing, holding a child, feeding some hens or chatting with a neighbour over the front gate. They are charming depictions of simple, domestic life that appeal to so many of us today because this seems like a world that is lost to us.

But I have to admit that one of my favourite thatched properties is one I've never actually seen let alone visited, and that's because it's fictional. Podmore's Thatch is the house that belongs to the heroine, Penelope Keeling, in Rosamunde Pilcher's bestselling novel, *The Shell Seekers*. The novel opens with Penelope in hospital. She's fed up and desperate to return to her beloved home and garden and so discharges herself and we soon see her happily working in her flower beds, much to the chagrin of her daughter, Nancy.

Then there's Tyler's Row – the thatched cottages that feature in one of Miss Read's Fairacre novels. Bought by a couple who fall for its picturesque features and its country setting, they soon find there's plenty of work to do, fixing the old electrics, plumbing and rotting window frames.

Thatched cottages are very often picturesque and none more so than the 'cottage orné' – a style of home popular in the late eighteenth and early nineteenth-century. They were built to delight the eye with their shapely, curving roofs and ornate windows and doors. When I read about these curious buildings, I remembered one from my childhood that sat beside a village church. It looked so fairytale-like with its Gothic windows and curved flint walls under its low thatch, and I was always desperate to see inside it.

I wonder what it is about thatched properties that inspires such great affection. They do always look so very homely with their thick roofs, tiny windows and pretty gardens, and they're often the first thing people picture when asked to describe the quintessential English country home. But what will the reality of living in one be like? Roy keeps teasing me, saying we'll probably only live in it for five years before pronouncing it too cold and draughty and moving into a brand new eco-house.

But could we ever really live in a new build? A home that doesn't have a history is hard for me to imagine. Maybe we could compromise on a barn conversion so that it retains some of the character of an old building with its wonderful beams, but with some of the latest modern conveniences. But I do wonder if we're actually meant to be mollycoddled like this in our homes. We've become so used to shutting ourselves away from the weather and cranking the heating up. Now, I feel the cold – believe me – I really do. I suffer from Raynaud's – a condition which means my hands and feet are often painfully cold. However, I kind of think that a few draughts can't really do you much harm. It keeps buildings naturally aired, chasing away damp and germs. But perhaps a couple of winters in Old Thatch might change our minds although, at this stage, it's hard to imagine.

Thatch is a fascinating material. Ours is a reed thatch which lasts longer than straw thatch which is laid thicker but looser. When reed thatch erodes, it is usually stripped right back to the rafters and the thatch is completely replaced whereas straw thatch tends to be just topped up over the previous layer.

One of the things that puts most people off owning a thatched property, and certainly gave us pause for thought, is the risk of fire. We've seen the devastation it can cause. Just a few years ago, a beautiful thatched cottage in a nearby village caught fire. It was heartbreaking to see. It's no coincidence that thatched properties were banned from cities in the seventeenth-century after the Fire of London. Indeed, London itself had banned thatch in 1212 after a devastating fire claimed 3,000 lives. The close proximity of this combustible material in cities meant that fires could spread at ferocious and unstoppable speeds. But it's easier to take precautions in the country and owners of thatched properties are often far more vigilant with things like sweeping chimneys, smoke detectors, electrical surveys etc than those in more traditional properties, thus ensuring the best possible safety. Still, insuring a thatched home is expensive. One company we looked at for insurance provides cover not only for those living in thatched houses, but also for bankrupts and those with criminal records. Owning a thatch seems like a special kind of notoriety.

There are other things to consider with a thatched property too. As a material, thatch isn't just attractive to us humans – it's pretty attractive to animals too. Wire is placed over the thatch to prevent birds stealing it for their nests or, indeed, nesting inside the thatched roof but, alas, some birds do manage to get through the wire and then can't get themselves out. This happened when I was house-sitting a thatched property once. I was woken up early one morning by the oddest sound and it took me a while to identify what it was. I opened the bedroom window which was directly beneath the eaves of the thatch and, looking up and along the length of it, I saw a little sparrow marching up and down, obviously trying to find a way out of the wire maze he'd got himself into. I left him to it, but he was still marching hours later and I became anxious that the poor creature would wear himself out. But he had got in so, surely, there was a way out.

I carefully placed a bit of bread inside the thatch for him, but he didn't eat it and was still marching after I'd walked around the property to see if there was a sparrow-sized gap anywhere that I could somehow coax him towards. But there wasn't. There was only one solution – to cut the wire! I found some secateurs and did the deed and the bird escaped much to my relief and I did a little patch job with the wire.

Birds do love thatch. One morning, I stepped out of the shower at Old Thatch and opened the small casement window and I was soon aware of being watched as I got dressed. The cheeky red face of a goldfinch was staring right at me and it was soon followed by its partner. The first one fixed its eyes on me, giving a high-pitched *twit-twit*. Its partner flew away, but then a blue tit landed on the thatch. Were they, perhaps, looking for nesting material? I really should have shooed them away in case they started pulling the reed from our roof, but I didn't the heart. There was plenty of reed there for all of us, I decided.

Decide on Your Area

Now that we're here at Old Thatch, there seems a strange kind of inevitability about it all. I remember, when we started looking at properties, studying an online map and trying to work out the areas we favoured. We didn't want to go far. We loved the little pocket of Suffolk we'd found with its pretty woods and valleys. Plus it had the advantage of not being too far away from good train links to London for Roy to visit art exhibitions.

The general advice when moving seems to be that you should decide on your area and not budge. Well, we knew the area we loved and there were a handful of villages in particular that we adored and just kept coming back to. Especially one. It was a village I discovered shortly after coming to Suffolk, while exploring the many footpaths that wended through the valleys, passing ancient churches with towers and steeples, bluebell woods and old farmyards full of geese. There was something about it that I felt in my heart.

It's funny, this notion of a place having the 'right feel'. I think it was a good seven or eight years before we found Old Thatch that I really fell in love with this particular area, frequenting it on walks with friends, visiting its churches, photographing the villages, the footpaths and the river and dreaming of what it would be like to live here.

When we took Hattie for a walk after viewing Old Thatch for the first time, we found a little lane that dipped into the valley, passing a few well-detached homes including a couple of characterful farmhouses. It wasn't until we turned around and were coming back up the lane that something struck me – this lane, this part of the village, reminded me of a book cover from a novel I'd read back in the mid-nineties. It was one of those wonderful so-called 'Aga Sagas' that were all the rage back then – country-set novels about rural lives. I lapped them up and there was one that had the prettiest cover.

I was living in a rather grim basement flat in the market town of Skipton in North Yorkshire, but I had great aspirations to move out to one of the neighbouring villages and to live in a pretty cottage. Alas, my meagre civil servant salary didn't allow that at the time and the dream had to remain a dream. But here, in this little Suffolk lane, almost twenty-five years later, I began to think I might have found what I was looking for back then. The lane doesn't look exactly like the one on the cover of that novel, but there's something about it that gave me exactly the same feeling I'd had all those years ago when I was looking at it – one of peace, joy and happiness.

I had found the place I wanted to be.

Country Living

I knew from a young age that peace, at least for me, came from the countryside, and not just the peace that comes from no noise. If anything, the countryside can be filled with noise from the lowing of cows and bleating of sheep to the high speed tractors and joyriders who terrorise the little lanes. But there's another level of peace – that wondrous deep peace that comes from within when you find yourself in an environment that you truly love.

I was lucky that I grew up in the rural villages of Norfolk and a lot of my free time was spent outdoors. One of the fondest memories I have from my childhood is the simple pleasure of a bike ride, particularly if there was the promise of some juicy strawberries at the end of it. We never lived far from strawberry fields and it used to be an easy way for a teenager to make a bit of money. So I'd cycle over to the fields, meeting up with a friend, and we'd spend the whole day picking strawberries. One day, when it was much too hot to work, we'd take breaks, sitting in the shade of the hedge, gossiping. Not a lot of strawberries got picked that day, but it was a wonderful time spent outdoors with my companion.

Another joy of country living is the wildlife. We're very lucky to have more than our share of barn owls in the Suffolk countryside. One of our neighbours at Mulberry Cottage owned seventy acres of land and had built a straw bale barn owl tower. It really was something special and it had regular residents too, who were glorious to see flying across the valley at twilight. There was also a barn owl box in one of the fields in the village and Hattie and I would often see an owl on our afternoon walks in winter when it would be out hunting in the meadows, its silent flight holding you captive.

It's so important to be aware of the environment around us and to protect it. Alas, this isn't always at the forefront of a developer's mind. Just before we left Mulberry Cottage, a row of new houses was built opposite a thatched cottage as you enter the village. We were talking to the owner of one of the new homes on a morning walk. She was delighted by the resident owls.

'They come so close,' she enthused. 'They sit on our garden fence.'

I was amazed to hear this and then I remembered that the land the houses had been built on had been a meadow for years before that and was very likely the owl's favoured haunt. It was probably sitting on the fence bemused by what had happened to its field.

Something we're looking forward to at Old Thatch is getting to know the local walks. There's little I enjoy more than exploring the network of footpaths our countryside boasts. I can happily lose myself for hours, taking a left here, a right there, crossing fields and dipping into woods. On the first really sunny day after moving we venture forth, fully embracing the day. We cross the green which is studded with early daisies, dandelions and daffodils, then pass a farmhouse whose garden boasts the loveliest pale pink blossom, so bright against the blue sky. We follow a narrow dead-end lane down into the valley and find an old wooden stile into a field. It's muddy after all the rain and we're glad of our sturdy wellies as we follow the path. It leads to a little river and we discover two wild cherry trees in blossom by its banks. We let Hattie off her lead here. It's safely away from roads and there is no livestock to worry. She makes the most of her freedom and, when we call her back to us, she's turned into a mud monster, caked but happy.

We follow the river, pausing to watch at a bend as we notice a branch sticking out of the water.

'Good spot for a kingfisher,' I say. Roy agrees. He was thinking exactly the same thing. He spots it first a second later. That unmistakable flash of blue and orange. We gasp. It's only there above the water for a moment before it flies across the field, but we saw it. We were there at just the right moment, focusing our attention on just the right spot. It's as if we conjured it up out of sheer willpower.

The path continues to get muddier for a while before coming out on a little lane which has a long island of thick pockmarked mud down the middle of it. It leads to a ford and there's a small field where a woman is pushing a wheel barrow with a large bag of horse feed. There are two horses – a chestnut and a piebald – who greet her with enthusiasm and we stop to say hello by the gate, asking where the footpaths go. As she tells us, the piebald eagerly strikes the wheelbarrow with his large, fetlocked hoof, tipping it over a moment later. Now, the horse hits the bag with great persistence. The owner is aware. It's nothing new, but we're amazed to see this, laughing when the bag of feed finally splits open and the horse can claim its reward.

We walk on, entering another field via a slippery bank, spying a thatched cottage with a sweet garden. The high path skirts it and we're able to look down into the garden which is wonderful for a nosy writer like me – I adore getting a glimpse of other people's lives, but I'm aware of how it wouldn't suit me at all if I lived there. When I'm in my garden, I'm in a world of my own as I sow my seeds and tend my plants and the very last thing I'd want is a couple of strangers' heads bobbing over the hedge.

We find ourselves back on the little lane we left a few minutes ago and follow the hill to the next footpath which crosses the field back to our village. It's a beautiful circular walk and I can't help wondering how many times we'll enjoy it over the coming months and years, getting to know it slowly, through each of the seasons, delighting in the many little changes while meeting more neighbours and, minute by minute, feeling more at home.

The next day, the blue skies have been replaced by grey again. It's the spring equinox, but it feels more like we've been plunged back into the depths of winter. It isn't the kind of day you want to discover that your Aga has mysteriously switched itself off and is now nothing more than a giant frozen piece of enamel in the kitchen. Nor is it the kind of day you want to have to open all your windows because of Covid and the safety precautions we're advised to take when trades people visit. But it's a requirement of the insurance on our thatched property that we have an electrical test done periodically. It's deeply frustrating that it's due within a week of us moving in as the house is still full of boxes and we're not even sure where all the sockets are.

I sit on the sofa with my laptop, a hot water bottle secured in the layers of my clothing and a cup of tea beside me. We have quickly come to understand why so many old buildings have Agas in their kitchens because, as soon as ours goes out, the room loses its essence as well as its warmth. The kitchen is dual aspect, with three single-glazed windows, and the cold March air is felt in full force. It's quite miserable as there is no other heating in this room and the floor is cold slate. Roy gets to work, trying to find out what's wrong with the Aga and we have it back on in a few days. And then the boiler breaks. It's Friday. Of course it's Friday – the only day when boilers seem to break down. Thank goodness we have the Aga working again because, other than that, and a plug-in heater in the living room and the downstairs electric shower, we have no heating. It would have been easy to cope with in the summer months, but Old Thatch is an old house and it's a particularly cold spell, the wind coming viciously from the north. We've quickly discovered that our home heats up pretty quickly when you put the heating on, but that it doesn't retain the heat well as the walls are thin and poorly insulated and the single-glazed windows are no barrier at all, pretty though they are.

So we spend a few days shivering around the house and I spend as much time as I can in the greenhouse which heats up wonderfully even if there's only a little bit of sun around. It's very pleasant to be there, surrounded by my packets of seeds and bags of compost. It's only when I come back inside and have to wash my gardener's hands in cold water that I remember the predicament we're in.

We get in touch with a builder friend and ask if he knows anyone who might be able to fix our boiler and he gives us the name of a chap who comes round after the bank holiday weekend. Luckily, he's able to fix it and we have heat and hot water once again. We quickly ask his advice on some of the other issues at Old Thatch. It's quite a list and he determines that he'll need to book us in for a whole day.

Getting Back to Nature

We live so much of our lives indoors. At least, I know I do. Even though I adore my garden and the countryside, I still spend the majority of my waking hours staring at a computer screen. Maybe it's because I love my job as a writer. When I'm in the full flow of a novel, telling myself the story for the first time during that magical first draft stage, I find it hard to down tools. But years of working this way have caught up with me and backache, shoulder pain, eye strain and headaches mean that I have to learn to balance my days better. I have to take more breaks. And this is something I promise myself I'll do at Old Thatch.

There are so many things I want to incorporate into my life here. I want to create a new vegetable garden, making half a dozen new beds in which to grow fruit, vegetables and flowers. I want to cook and preserve more produce from the garden including more herbs, and learn how to make balms and lotions.

I want to be much more aware of not just the passing seasons, but the passing months. One way of doing this is to moon watch – observing the waxing and the waning, the crescent moon and the full moon. There are some gardeners who believe in the power of the moon and sow, plant and harvest by its phases. This interests me too.

I vow to go for more walks and, one afternoon, after a session both at my computer and in the garden, I take myself off for the little circuit from our village into the valley. The light is beautiful, the sun flitting in and out of gentle clouds. The lanes are green and thick with young Alexanders which are chartreuse in colour – vibrant and glowing with health and vigour. These, I'm told by a friend who loves to make dyes from plants, is the first dye plant of the year, much loved by the Romans who brought it over with them and called it 'pot herb of Alexandria'. Another gardening friend tells me they are good in tempura and I soon discover that every part of the plant is edible.

I turn down a one-track lane, noticing the mountains of brambles on either side which no doubt threaten to swallow the road completely come summertime. I spot a buzzard and a pair of geese calling as they fly with such surety high above me. I wonder where they're going. They seem far more certain and determined than I do.

I follow the footpath into the field, but then I falter as another field opens to my right. Which way is the right way? Many years ago, when I was writing novels for children, I wrote a book called *Collingwood Castle* in which there was a character called 'Farmer Oi' because that was the cry he'd give on seeing anybody crossing his land. Well, it seems that my fictional Farmer Oi has come to life in our little community for there is indeed a farmer who owns some of the fields in the neighbourhood and he hates dog walkers. We're told this by several people before Roy meets him one day, driving a very old tractor. He slows down and Roy introduces himself.

'Glad to see you've got your dog on a lead,' Farmer Oi tells Roy. 'You might have heard I'm not popular round here. Don't like dogs off lead on my land.' He raises his arms and mimes pointing a gun.

It's this that I'm thinking of as I try and guess which path is the footpath. I wouldn't like my first encounter with Farmer Oi to be a negative one. I choose right and, soon, the path joins one that we've already walked down and I know where I am.

I climb over a steep stile. I wonder if it's the work of Farmer Oi because it's not user-friendly and takes a bit of working out to get your whole body over it without toppling backwards or forwards or leaving a leg behind. I then cross a pretty field where there's a huge rabbit warren, spotting the young bunnies as they run for cover.

I come out on the lane near our cottage, passing the old farmhouse on the green where Graham lives. Graham on the Green, I call him. He's a lovely retired gentleman and is often out in his garden. Indeed, he can often be seen pottering in and out, keeping an eye on things and is always happy to chat to passers-by. His dog also sounds the alarm if anybody walks by, and I think its owner welcomes this chance to catch up on a bit of gossip. He doesn't want to miss anybody. But Graham on the Green isn't out today and so I return home.

One of the loveliest things about Old Thatch is that it backs on to our neighbour's meadow and there are fields and woods beyond that. It's a beautiful open horizon and we're not the only ones to enjoy it. Every day, we can hear skylarks over the meadow, their spiralling song always uplifting. We also often hear a buzzard from the bathroom. It is a true joy to be able to hear birdsong from every room in the house.

Spring Comes Slowly

During our first month at Old Thatch, we have a lot of flat, grey days where the sun – if it appears at all – is weak and fleeting. But it doesn't stop spring's progress and I watch in anticipation as buds burst forth in the garden and shoots push through the earth. It's incredibly exciting as we wait to discover just what the garden has in store for us. In one of the front borders, deep red shoots appear. Is it a peony? Please let it be pink or white! And is that a cherry tree? Are those irises? I'm pretty sure there are tulips in one of the borders, but what colour will they be? Will we have bluebells? Camassias? I've already spotted the rugosa roses and I'm so happy to see these as we left a hedge of these roses at Mulberry Cottage and it broke my heart to lose them. We'd planted them when they were small and they were over five foot tall when we left, but they were far too thorny to dig up or even to take cuttings from. But what variety will these be?

I took lots of photos during our viewing back in the summer so I can look at some of these for reference, but they are only little pockets of the garden and I haven't managed to capture everything. I'm quite glad of this because it will be a wonderful surprise as the year unfolds, the garden sharing its secrets with us. Of course, this also means that I'm limited when it comes to planting new things in the existing beds because I'm not sure what's already in there. The answer to this is to create brand new beds which is exactly what I'm planning, including a circular rose border at the front of the cottage for some of the rose cuttings I took. It should look gorgeous. Delicate peachy pink roses which will be interspersed with herbs, perhaps – some vivid purple anise hyssop, and some white cosmos during the summer months.

We are thrilled to discover a magnolia tree at Old Thatch and there's the almost unbearable joy of seeing the flowers unfurling. When they finally do, the vivid blue of the April sky is the perfect backdrop and, for about four days, it looks perfect. And then the frost comes, cruel and swift, it steals the beauty from our tree and the others in the neighbourhood, leaving soggy brown petals behind. I want to punch the weather for this brutal blow, but later flowers bloom so all is not lost.

Another almost painful joy is the slow progress of the wisteria. I'll never forget my excitement at seeing the buds for the first time, watching as they slowly elongate and then open, showing more of their deep purple beauty each day.

We also wait in anticipation to see fruit form on the apple and cherry trees, planning recipes and wondering how many of them we can cook in the Aga when we turn it on again in the darker days of autumn, and how much food we can store over the long winter months, each mouthful reminding us of the long, warm days of summer. There is so much to look forward to.

It's very easy while living at Old Thatch to forget the outside world. Other than trips to the shop for food, we're quite happy to spend weeks at a time without going anywhere. Indeed, the Covid pandemic has trained us well to do this. But, even before the pandemic, my husband and I were both able to work quietly from home, happy in each other's company, without the need to go out. And, for the first five weeks at Old Thatch, we really are cut off from the world as we have no proper internet connection other than via Roy's phone. So, every time I want to check my email or go online, I have to ask him to hook me up. It really makes you stop and think if you absolutely need to go online at any given time. Rather than just mindlessly logging on to one of the social media sites and losing countless minutes to scrolling the latest photos and gossip, your time opens up to you and, instead of updating your statuses on three different platforms, uploading photo after photo, commenting, liking and refreshing, you find yourself with all these extra minutes, hours. I pick up a book. I potter in the garden. I go for a walk.

I start reading through the wonderful cookbooks and gardening books I have. Many are about the joys of foraging as well as growing your own food and I remember seeing our local lanes lined with Alexanders. I've never eaten any, but I look them up and decide that this will be my first foraged food gathered at Old Thatch. Roy isn't so sure, anxious that the plants might not actually be Alexanders. After all, they're usually found by the coast, aren't they? What are they doing so far inland? But I'm pretty sure I've identified them correctly and take off with secateurs and a carrier bag the next day, choosing a spot on a lane unfrequented by traffic, high on the verge away from where dogs might be tempted to lift a leg, yet not too close to fields which farmers might have sprayed with pesticides. It's quite a list of things to remember.

Then there's the plant itself. The Alexanders have been flourishing for a few weeks now and some of them are most definitely past their best, drooping and browning in the spring sunshine. So I'm careful to choose the youngest, freshest plants – cutting the pretty yellow-green dome-shaped flowers, the ridged stems and the glossy leaves as all are edible.

Once home, I wash my foraged goodies thoroughly, checking everything again for signs of browning. Then we cook it all in a pan on the Aga for a good ten minutes. You can eat it just like asparagus and so we serve it simply with butter and salt. And it's delicious. I can't actually believe how good it is. No wonder the Romans brought it over with them. This is prime greens and there is plenty of it freely available right on our doorstep. And I can't think of a better way of getting to know your environment and being a part of it than by eating it. And who knows what else we'll discover in the countryside around us as well as in our own garden. Spring is just the beginning.

Sunday Walks

We have always found that dog walking is a great way to meet people. Back in the London suburbs, I truly believe that I would never have met anyone in our road or in the neighbourhood if I hadn't been out with Molly, our spaniel. Even though we lived in a long terrace, people didn't tend to chat much. You rarely saw your neighbours. Now, in Suffolk, we know that if we go out on a dog walk, especially on a Sunday, we will meet no end of people.

There's one particular Sunday I remember with fondness. We'd left our cottage on a bright spring morning, our neighbours' gardens studded with primroses and tulips, the blackthorn bright and snowy in the hedges. We climbed two of Farmer Oi's tricky stiles, deeming this better than a workout at a gym, before following the field down to the river. It was quiet and we didn't see anybody until we walked back on to a lane and saw a woman with two dogs coming towards us. The smaller of the two, a terrier, was off lead and started barking at us while the larger, a lurcher, was on an extending lead which immediately wrapped around Roy's legs. As the owner did her best to release him, the dog wound itself around me and I became entangled.

'Oh, dear!' she cried. 'It's okay. We're nearly there.'

Finally, we got untangled. Well, that's one way to meet somebody, I thought with a smile. We introduced ourselves. She lived in an ancient house in the next village – one I'd already spotted because of its marvellous old mullioned windows. We talked about the local farmers. Roy had already met Farmer Oi. But the other sounded kinder to walkers, keeping an unofficial footpath clear at the end of one of his fields which linked one footpath to another and which the locals often used. If the field belonged to Farmer Oi, we doubted he'd do the same. We'd already experienced the tricky stiles, but we'd also found footpath signs in heaps of brambles, and the circular signs on stiles having been chipped away. So it's just as well to know whose land you're walking across, we mused.

As we were about to say our goodbyes and continue on our walk, a woman came out of the thatched cottage on the lane and we were introduced to her.

'Welcome to our little corner of Suffolk,' she said when we told her we'd just moved here. We chatted for a bit and then she pointed to a man who'd just come out of the cottage next to hers.

'That's Martin,' she told us and so we started chatting to him. Poor Hattie was getting very fed up by this stage, wondering if this walk of ours was ever going to actually involve walking. But we were having so much fun getting to know people.

Martin told us that he had no fewer than three springs in his cottage garden. When he'd dug his pond, he'd simply left it to fill up naturally. He told us of further plans he had for the garden and we told him about the 'no-dig' beds we were creating.

'Well, if you need any earth, feel free to take some of mine. There'll be plenty going spare.'

We thanked him and explained that we'd just had two tonnes delivered so we probably had enough.

We finally continued our walk, much to Hattie's relief, following the lane back to a footpath that cuts across a field towards our cottage. It had been a wonderful morning meeting everyone and their dogs. I only hoped we'd remember everyone's name.

How lucky we felt to have found this community. Indeed, we'd received so many cards of welcome from neighbours. It was really touching and it went completely against everything you hear about small country communities not being welcoming. We couldn't have been made to feel more at home.

Aga Love

We would never have bought an Aga. Although we can see the beauty of them and have enjoyed cooking on other people's Agas over the years, the thought of having a huge fuel-guzzling cooker on twenty-four hours a day doesn't sit right with us. It seems too extravagant, too wasteful. And yet I couldn't help being just a little bit thrilled by the fact that there was a shiny blue Aga at Old Thatch. Dating from the seventies, we believe, it stands proud at the heart of the kitchen, imbuing the room with its warmth, ready to defrost your frozen limbs, dry your washing or even cook you a meal!

Well, we thought, there was no point in getting rid of it as it could be incredibly expensive to move an Aga, so we vowed to enjoy using it. It would be one of life's little adventures. But it would most certainly be switched off come late spring.

And then the purchases began. We'd need new baking trays that fitted neatly on its runners. We'd need a proper Aga kettle, we said, promptly choosing one in volcanic orange to match a pan and an oven dish we already had. And we'd most definitely need a toast bat – one of those delightful racket-like implements which toasts bread to perfection.

The Aga was designed by a Nobel prize-winning Swedish physicist in 1922. As soon as I knew we were going to be the owners of one, I joined two Facebook Aga groups and started reading the posts. These people are passionate about their Agas. They're more than just cookers – they're a member of the family, the heart of the home. But they aren't the easiest things to use when you're not used to them. The Facebook groups are full of questions about how to cook things correctly because you can't control an Aga's temperature easily and, as soon as you use the enormous hot plates, heat is lost from the ovens so you have to account for that when you're cooking. It's quite an art and I worry that I won't be able to master it.

The first time I use the heavy orange kettle on one of the hot plates, I'm a little anxious. I'm so used to our electric kettle and how fast that is. The Aga one takes more than double the time to heat up, but how pretty it looks, I think, falling in love with the bright orange on top of the glossy blue cooker. It's a whistling kettle and Roy and I are looking forward to hearing it for the first time. But, rather than having a clear, clean whistle, it stutters and whines. It sounds like the wind at Wuthering Heights, but it makes me smile. There's definitely no mistaking it at least.

Our sellers left us some old Aga handbooks and cookbooks and we have fun looking through them. Roy finds a recipe for a Magic Lemon Cake and it is glorious – sunshine in a dish, it's the runniest, lemoniest concoction ever and it doesn't take us long to eat the lot. I slowly get used to making all my favourite things without turning to a regular oven, constantly checking progress in case I burn things. We have a two-door Aga with a roasting oven and a warming oven. There are two hot plates, each with massive, heavy silver lids which you would not want to drop on your hands. A chrome rail at the front is used for tea towels and our oven gloves and gauntlet, but we soon find ourselves draping damp clothes on it and warming socks and gloves. We are clearly turning into Aga owners.

Next to the kitchen, we have a beautiful dining room with an enormous inglenook fireplace and French doors out into the garden. We've put our old oak settle and dining table here, but we have yet to eat there, preferring our scruffy little table with makeshift chairs that we've placed in the kitchen, enjoying the companionship of the Aga as we eat, its gentle warmth making everything taste better.

When we first viewed Old Thatch, we noticed that there was a dog bed next to the Aga. This seems to be a popular thing with those who own both Agas and dogs. So we do the same, placing one of Hattie's baskets next to it. But she isn't interested. She likes the dining room, the living room, the mat by the back door or a patch of carpet in my study where the sun falls. But she doesn't much care for the Aga. Until one day. I was settled at our little table with my laptop and a cup of tea made using the Wuthering Heights kettle when it happened. Hattie came in, crossed the room and settled down by the Aga. Not in the basket, mind, but in front of the cooker. I watched as she curled herself up and, slowly, her eyes closed in contentment as she, like us, discovered the great joy of having an Aga in the family.

One morning over the cold Easter weekend, I come through to the kitchen and see the shiny new enamel kettle sitting on the Aga and the long oven glove we bought hanging from the chrome rail. Roy has a pan of porridge warming on one of the hot plates and the rosemary focaccia he made the day before is sitting on the countertop along with the glass jar of his sourdough starter, and I've left a recipe out for vegan samosas which we'll make for lunch today. I smile to myself. We really didn't believe that we would love the Aga so much, but it's pretty much the focus of our day as we plan meals and keep warm around it, and I'm so happy that this one found its way into our lives.

Wildlife

One of the things I love most about Old Thatch is the wildlife. When we first moved in, we were amazed by the number of ladybirds everywhere – not just in the garden but also in the house, favouring the windowsills. This bodes well because ladybirds are great allies of gardeners, eating all sorts of nasty things like aphids and other pests.

We also have a garden full of birds and there is so much birdsong from the rich notes of blackbirds, to the happy song of the robins, the manic twitter of goldfinches and the heaven-piercing notes of the skylarks. We can hear them all from inside. Indeed, it's sometimes hard to tell the difference between outside and inside. Old Thatch sits centrally in its plot of garden and, as such, the garden feels all-present. We can see it from every single window – some of our rooms giving us three different views of it. So it's easy to watch what's happening outside which isn't always a benefit, I quickly learn.

Our neighbour tells us that we have a resident sparrowhawk. This impresses us until he says that it waits for birds by the bird feeder, watching them and then attacking when they fly into a nearby hedge. But, as I haven't seen this myself, I try and put it from my mind. Nothing like that will happen at Old Thatch, will it?

Then one morning, I'm working in the conservatory, writing at my laptop and in a world of my own, when I become aware of the distress cry of a blackbird. It doesn't sound normal. I open the door into the garden, trying to find out where it's coming from and that's when I see the sparrowhawk on the ground in our meadow, its great talons resting on a male blackbird who is struggling to get free, its pitiful cries are heart-wrenching. I'm frozen for a moment. What can I do? Is it too late? If I scare the sparrowhawk off, will the blackbird be left mortally wounded? I don't want to have to see that and so I leave it for a few seconds, hoping the bird of prey will kill the blackbird quickly and mercifully, only it doesn't, and the blackbird is still struggling. I decide to take action and walk outside, feeling certain I'll scare the hawk away and the blackbird will be freed. But I'm in for a surprise as the sparrowhawk takes off, lifting the blackbird with it and flying over a neighbour's hedge. I stand motionless, my heart breaking for the blackbird. It's probably one of the ones I've been watching on our front lawn. Maybe it was even one of the birds that has been singing as I garden late into the evening.

I go back inside. I've had quite enough wildlife for one day.

Another evening, I see the hawk on the lawn near the back door, feasting on some poor creature. When we examine the site afterwards, we find a little patch of fur and guess Old Thatch must have lost a resident mouse.

There is a little path that leads from the front garden to the back between the house and garage. It's a handy cut-through and saves a bit of a walk, but we determine not to use it as soon as we discover a robin's nest in the thick foliage growing up the garage wall. It's a beautiful, open nest, easily visible, and there appears to be just one baby bird inside.

In another hedge near the greenhouse there's a blackbird's nest, but it's too high up to see inside although I do see the mother one evening when I take a peep. She stares back at me and I quickly leave her to it, muttering an apology. Humans have no business poking into hedgerows come spring, I think, chiding myself for my nosiness.

I can sit and watch the birds for hours. The robin and blackbird are relentless hunters while feeding their young and I see them on the lawns, in our borders and flitting from our trees. One evening, there's a robin sitting in the heart of our blackthorn, the red of its breast so vivid against the white blossom. Is it our nesting robin, I wonder? Do busy parents have time to sing?

It's a wonderful gift when moving house to discover that you are sharing your space with all these other lives and, even if the resident moles are in the process of making rather a mess of our little meadow, it's hard to begrudge them a small corner of our new home.

The M R James Connection

I can't remember how I first heard about M R James, but I became more aware of him once we moved to Suffolk. The famous writer of ghost stories was born in the county and I was intrigued enough about him to watch a documentary by Mark Gatiss. That, in turn, led me to find out about Robert Lloyd Parry who gives the most remarkable performances, reciting James's ghost stories in atmospheric settings.

One such performance Roy and I were lucky enough to attend was on a cold winter's evening at one of the oldest houses in the country – The Manor at Hemingford Grey in Cambridgeshire. Built in the twelfth century and once owned by the author Lucy Boston, it was made famous through her Children of Green Knowe stories. I was so excited to visit but, as it was dark, we couldn't see the famous topiary garden. But the house didn't disappoint. One of its quirks was, to get to the oldest room in the ancient building, we had to pass through the current owner's bedroom. Diana Boston is the daughter-in-law of Lucy Boston and couldn't have made the small audience more welcome, giving us drinks and telling us a little of the history of the place.

And then the performance began, with Robert Lloyd Parry dressed as M R James with neat round glasses, hair slicked back, and waistcoat with watch chain. There was a candle on a small table beside the great winged chair he occupied. He treated us to two ghost stories by candlelight that evening and I think it was made all the more atmospheric because of the intense cold for there was no heating in the room – at all.

My fascination with M R James was well and truly ignited. Next, we had a trip to King's College in Cambridge where James was provost and taught for many years, reading his stories out loud to lucky students on Christmas Eve.

I found a copy of James's book, *Suffolk and Norfolk*, in which he details some of his favourite churches in the two neighbouring counties, and this has provided us with many wonderful days out. It's a treat to be able to follow in a great writer's footsteps, seeing the places he loved and observing some of the things that might have inspired his fiction, including the old rectory at Great Livermere where he grew up and the church where his father was rector.

One of my friends, I discover, is a fellow James fan and she says she'll lend me two books she has. I'm astounded as she hands the wonderful old hardbacks to me in the changing rooms before we go swimming one day. This doesn't feel like the right setting to handle such precious tomes and putting them into a gym locker feels so wrong.

Later, we venture to the church that features in one of the stories, *Count Magnus*. As is befitting, it's a bleak, steely sort of day, just the kind when you may stumble upon two ghostly figures at a country crossroads. With all of this feeding my imagination, I know I want to write about it somehow and *Christmas with the Book Lovers* is born – the premise being, can a book be haunted? It gives me free rein to invent a few ghost stories of my own as the book-loving Nightingale family sit around the fireplace on Christmas Eve in true Victorian fashion, telling ghost stories just as James himself did.

I also use this book to explore another East Anglian myth –

that of Black Shuck - the large, dark demon dog who terrorises the countryside and whose presence is believed to forewarn of a death. Roy and I have already explored some of Black Shuck's haunts including the magnificent church at Blythburgh near the coast. It stands tall and proud above the marshy countryside and is famous for its carved angels which gaze down upon its congregation. But it's also famous for the tale of Shuck who, during a thunderstorm in 1577, killed worshippers in the church. Dark scorch marks can clearly be seen on one of the large wooden doors. Claw marks of the beast, perhaps.

It's a delightfully dark and grisly story. But is it true?

Just a few years ago, the bones of a large dog, believing to date back to the sixteenth-century, were discovered at nearby Leiston Abbey. Could this be Shuck? Is this proof that he really existed? It's fun to speculate, but the storyteller in me doesn't need hard facts. Myths don't need to be rooted in the truth. As long as it's a good story, that's enough.

When we found Old Thatch, I immediately looked up two churches near us and I'm delighted to discover that both feature in M R James's *Suffolk and Norfolk* book. He notes the fine porch and font at one of them and the carved door at the other but, alas, like so many of East Anglia's churches, the latter has been decimated by William 'Basher' Dowsing who, during the English Civil War, did so much damage to our churches, removing and destroying relics, altar rails, paintings, windows and so much more.

It's frustrating that so many local treasures have been lost to us through this legalised vandalism but there is still plenty to enjoy today and we feel very lucky that we have so many beautiful churches around us.

One question we get asked all the time is if Old Thatch is haunted. It's easy to imagine that it could be because of its age and there are definitely some spooky dark corners around the fireplaces and plenty of odd creaks and groans. One thing we've noticed is that paintings and pictures hanging on the walls are always on the move, sliding ever-so-slightly so that they look almost permanently wonky. I'm sure there'll be an explanation for this, but we haven't found it yet. And what would we do if we did see a ghost? I like to think that I would be more curious than afraid, and hope that it would answer all the questions I'd have for it. Maybe we could become good friends like Carys and Georgiana in my novel, *Three Graces*. Maybe we could even write a novel together! But, for the present, Old Thatch seems to be a ghost-free zone.

A Word From a Fellow Thatch Owner

One of our artist friends, the talented Sara MacIver, also lives in a thatched cottage here in Suffolk and I wanted to share her thoughts with you. And, if you want to see her beautiful home, follow her on Instagram @suffolkcottage_stories.

Our thatch is rather like an eiderdown that wraps itself securely in a thick fold over our sixteenth-century cottage. Protecting from the storms, insulating in winter and cooling in summer, it is made from local materials, in this case, long straw and, being sustainable, it is appealing to an environmentally aware artist and her family.

The craft of thatching is an historical one, ages old and still in demand for the many thatched houses in the country. What better material than one that has been grown locally and uses no air miles to transport? It has a reassuring presence on an old clay lump cottage which is also built with local sustainable materials. A building created from the land it sits on.

Everything about the cottage is seasonal. The thatch (despite being covered in wire netting) will play host to wren's nests and sometimes the wild bees will tuck a small nest within. Doing very little harm, they are welcome visitors.

Most thatched houses are very old. With an old house comes a generous garden, and what drew me to our home was the idea that ours would support local wildlife and, if encouraged, it would develop its own biodiversity. I am a nature lover. Always have been. As a small child I would draw the insects I found in our field for school projects. The nature table was a 'thing' then and my favourite lessons were orientated around art and the natural world. I went on to take A-level art at school and the main subject was 'Plant Drawing'. Outside of my graphic design occupation, and sometimes within, I painted flowers. For greetings cards and packaging. So, you can imagine I will be a garden lover, growing and enjoying the flowers in our cottage garden.

When it rains you feel snug under the thatch, but the amazing thing is the comforting drip drip that follows after the rain has ceased. If you've had a spell of dry weather, the continuous drip delights as it waters the flower beds below. Long straw is laid in such a way as to encourage the rain to run off. Therefore, in winter when snow slowly thaws in sun, it creates the most spectacular icicles creating a scene out of Narnia. I was once asked by visitors to the village if it leaked! Ours is very thick, laid on top of the original thatch that serves as a record of the original materials as much as all the building's other features such as clay lump, wattle and daub and lime plaster. No, it does not leak and, if well maintained, it will last and be weather proof for many many years.

Sara MacIver

Home

Moving house is the most disconcerting feeling. There's the excitement – that wondrous sensation that you are embarking on a new chapter of your life. But what if you get it wrong? What if all your time and effort are misplaced and you find yourself living somewhere that doesn't give you that feeling of home?

I've lived in many different homes since childhood from a modern bungalow to an Edwardian house. I've lived in a noisy basement flat in a Victorian terrace in North Yorkshire and a 1930s suburban terrace in London. I've lived in a flat above somebody's garage in Worcestershire and spent one year in the spare bedroom at my grandfather's in Carlisle. But it wasn't until my husband and I moved to Suffolk that I really felt that sense of coming home. Suffolk, unlike the home counties, is still a relatively quiet place, sparsely populated compared to counties like Sussex and Kent. The country lanes are quiet, there are villages and hamlets that really do feel as if they're in the middle of nowhere, with no shops and, very often, a hopeless internet connection. It seems strange to us that a county with such beautiful countryside, stunning coastline and good links to London isn't more popular, but I have to say that I love it all the more because of that. It feels like a wonderful secret to us and, when we have visitors, they always seem surprised by how lovely it is and how little known.

But keep all this to yourself, won't you? I'm only telling you because I trust you as my reader.

Having found Old Thatch, it's hard to imagine living anywhere else now although the writer in me always wonders, what if... how about... maybe one day...? But I love the way this cottage came into our lives when we were most definitely not looking for a listed, timber-framed, thatched property. There it was, just waiting for us. Quietly unassuming, it didn't shout its presence, it simply wove itself into our hearts until we couldn't possibly think of any other property. And I finally have that deep sense of peace and belonging. It feels as if this house has been waiting for me. This is the place I've been moving towards my whole life.

End of Book One

Acknowledgements

Thank you to Roy, Catriona, Sara and Celia who all made wonderful contributions to this book.

About the Author

Victoria Connelly is the bestselling author of *The Rose Girls* and *The Book Lovers* series.

With over a million sales, her books have been translated into many languages. The first, *Flights of Angels*, was made into a film in Germany. Victoria flew to Berlin to see it being made and even played a cameo role in it.

A Weekend with Mr Darcy, the first in her popular Austen Addicts series about fans of Jane Austen has sold over 100,000 copies. She is also the author of several romantic comedies including *The Runaway Actress* which was nominated for the Romantic Novelists' Association's Best Romantic Comedy of the Year.

Victoria was brought up in Norfolk, England before moving to Yorkshire where she got married in a medieval castle. After 11 years in London, she moved to rural Suffolk where she lives in a thatched cottage with her artist husband, a springer spaniel and her ex-battery hens.

To hear about future releases and receive a **free ebook** sign up for her newsletter at www.victoriaconnelly.com.

Also by Victoria Connelly

The House in the Clouds Series

The House in the Clouds
High Blue Sky
The Colour of Summer

The Book Lovers Series

The Book Lovers
Rules for a Successful Book Club
Natural Born Readers
Scenes from a Country Bookshop
Christmas with the Book Lovers

Other Books

The Beauty of Broken Things
One Last Summer
The Heart of the Garden
Love in an English Garden

The Rose Girls

The Secret of You

Christmas at The Cove

Christmas at the Castle

Christmas at the Cottage

The Christmas Collection (A compilation volume)

A Summer to Remember

Wish You Were Here

The Runaway Actress

Molly's Millions

Flights of Angels

Irresistible You

Three Graces

It's Magic (A compilation volume)

A Weekend with Mr Darcy

The Perfect Hero (Dreaming of Mr Darcy)

Mr Darcy Forever

Christmas With Mr Darcy

Happy Birthday Mr Darcy

At Home with Mr Darcy

Escape to Mulberry Cottage (non-fiction)

A Year at Mulberry Cottage (non-fiction)

Summer at Mulberry Cottage (non-fiction)

Printed in Great Britain
by Amazon